Semiotic and Popular Culture Studies

Popular forms of entertainment have always existed. As he traveled the world, the ancient Greek historian Herodotus wrote about earthy, amusing performances and songs that seemed odd to him, but which were certainly very popular with common folk. He saw these, however, as the exception to the rule of true culture. One wonders what Herodotus would think in today's media culture, where his "exception" has become the rule. Why is popular culture so "popular"? What is psychologically behind it? What is it? Why do we hate to love it and love to hate it? What has happened to so-called high culture? What are the "meanings" and "social functions" of current pop culture forms such as sitcoms, reality TV programs, YouTube sites, and the like?

These are the kinds of questions that this series of books, written by experts and researchers in both popular culture studies and semiotics, will broach and discuss critically. Overall, they will attempt to decode the meanings inherent in spectacles, popular songs, coffee, video games, cars, fads, and other "objects" of contemporary pop culture. They will also take comprehensive glances at the relationship between culture and the human condition. Although written by scholars and intellectuals, each book will look beyond the many abstruse theories that have been put forward to explain popular culture, so as to penetrate its origins, evolution, and overall *raison d'être* human life, exploring the psychic structures that it expresses and which make it so profoundly appealing, even to those who claim to hate it. Pop culture has been *the* driving force in guiding, or at leashing shaping, social evolution since the Roaring Twenties, triggering a broad debate about art, sex, and "true culture" that is still ongoing. This debate is a crucial one in today's global village where traditional canons of art and aesthetics are being challenged as never before in human history.

The books are written in clear language and style so that readers of all backgrounds can understand what is going in pop culture theory and semiotics, and, thus reflect upon current cultural trends. They have the dual function of introducing various disciplinary attitudes and research findings in a user-friendly fashion so that they can be used as texts in colleges and universities, while still appeal to the interested general reader. Ultimately, the goal of each book is to provide a part of a generic semiotic framework for understanding the world we live in and probably will live in for the foreseeable future.

Marcel Danesi
University of Toronto

The Objects of Affection

Semiotics and Consumer Culture

Arthur Asa Berger

First published in 2010 by
PALGRAVE MACMILLAN®
in the United States—a division of St. Martin's Press LLC,
175 Fifth Avenue, New York, NY 10010.

Where this book is distributed in the UK, Europe and the rest of the world,
this is by Palgrave Macmillan, a division of Macmillan Publishers Limited,
registered in England, company number 785998, of Houndmills,
Basingstoke, Hampshire RG21 6XS.

Palgrave Macmillan is the global academic imprint of the above companies
and has companies and representatives throughout the world.

Palgrave® and Macmillan® are registered trademarks in the United States,
the United Kingdom, Europe and other countries.

ISBN: 978–0–230–10373–3

Library of Congress Cataloging-in-Publication Data

Berger, Arthur Asa, 1933–
    The objects of affection : semiotics and consumer culture / Arthur
Asa Berger.
        p. cm.—(Semiotics and popular culture)
    ISBN 978–0–230–10372–6 (hardback)
    ISBN 978–0–230–10373–3 (paperback)
        1. Semiotics—Social aspects. 2. Semiotics—Psychological aspects.
    3. Consumer behavior. 4. Material culture. 5. Object (Aesthetics)
    6. Culture—Semiotic models. 7. Language and culture. I. Title.

P99.4.S62B47 2010
302.2—dc22   2010001854

A catalogue record of the book is available from the British Library.

Design by Newgen Imaging Systems (P) Ltd., Chennai, India.

First edition: July 2010

D 10 9 8 7 6 5 4

Printed in the United States of America.

For my grandchildren:
Ariel, Kavanna, Seth, and Noah

Contents

Acknowledgments   xi

Part I   Semiotic Theory

1   The Science of Signs   **3**

The Semiotic Theories of Saussure and Peirce:
  An Overview   5
Some Contemporary Semiotic Theorists   11
Symbols   14
Denotation and Connotation   15
Metaphor and Metonymy   16
Language and Speech   20
Codes   23
Acura: An Example of Applied Semiotic Analysis   27
No Sign as a Sign   28
Signs within Signs   29
Signs That Lie   29

2   Consumer Cultures   **33**

Defining Consumer Cultures   34
The Sacred Origin of Consumer Cultures   36
Psychological Imperatives in Consumer Cultures   40
Marxist Theory and Consumer Cultures   42
Jean Baudrillard on Advertising and
  Consumer Cultures   46

3 Marketing Theory and Semiotics   **55**

Ernest Dichter and Motivation Research   56
Mary Douglas and Grid-Group Theory   58
New Strategist Publications   61
Claritas Explains That "Birds of a Feather
  Flock Together"   62
Complications for Marketers   68
Semiotics and Marketing Theory   69

Part II   Semiotic Applications

4 Brands and Identity: We Are Our Brands   **75**

Fashion and Identity   76
Semiotics and Brands   78
Style Choices and Identity   81
Hats   81
Hair   84
  Folklore, Myths, and Hair   85
  A Semiotic Approach to Hairstyles in the Eighties   86
  Blondeness: The Importance of Hair Color   87
Designer Eyeglasses and Sunglasses   88
Teeth   90
Wristwatches   92
Facial Hair in Men   95
Fragrances   97
  Brand Narcissism and L'Oréal Fragrances   98
Neckties   101
Shoes   104
Handbags and Messenger Bags   107
Brand Extensions and Lifestyle Signifiers   110
Style and the Postmodern Problematic   112

5 The Objects of Our Affection   **115**

Coffee   117
The Toaster   122
Swaddling Cloths   126
The "Evangelical" Hamburger   129

French-Fried Potatoes 131
Fountain Pens and Ink 134
Bikinis 136
Vodka 138
Beer 141
Veils 143
Cornflakes 145
White Bread 148
Bagels 151
Myst 153
Furniture 156
Teddy Bears 158
Soap Powders and Detergents 160
Vacuum Cleaners 162
Computers 164

6 **Learning Games and Activities** **169**
Time Capsule 169
Visit America Brochure 170
Your Brands and What They Reveal 171
Socioeconomic Classes and Brands 172
Automobiles and Personality 173
Spending Spree 173
Insights and Interesting Ideas 174

7 **Coda** **175**
The Origins of the Objects of Our Affection 175
The Complexity of Objects 177
People Watching and Artifact Analysis 178
The MP3 Shuffle and the Pastiche 180
The Semiotic Perspective and Being "Far Out" 181
Brands and the Self 182
Semiotics: It's Still With Me 183

Bibliography 185
Index 191

Acknowledgments

I would like to thank Marcel Danesi, the editor of this series, for including my book in this series and encouraging me when I was writing it. I met Marcel at an international conference on semiotics held at the University of California in Berkeley many years ago, and we've been in touch by email, off and on, since then. In 1963 I taught at the University of Milan and while there I met and had the chance to spend some time with Umberto Eco. We were both interested in comic strips at the time. His work on semiotics and culture has been an inspiration to me. My thanks, also, to my editor, Brigitte Shull, my editorial assistant Lee Norton, the production staff, the marketing staff, and everyone else who was involved with the publication of this book. I owe a debt of gratitude to the unnamed reviewers of this book, who offered numerous helpful suggestions for revising my manuscript, and a special debt of gratitude to Tom Doctoroff and Greg Rowland, who wrote blurbs for the book. Greg Rowland also sent a long and very useful email message with some suggestions that I utilized and from which I quoted several times in the book.

Previously Published Works

Li'l Abner, 1970 (Twayne); 1994 (Univ. of Mississippi Press)
The Evangelical Hamburger, 1970 (MSS Publications)
Pop Culture, 1973 (Pflaum)

About Man, 1974 (Pflaum)

The Comic-Stripped American, 1974 (Walker & Co., Penguin, Milano Libri)

The TV-Guided American, 1975 (Walker & Co.)

Language in Thought and Action (in collaboration with S. I. Hayakawa, author), 1974 (Harcourt Brace Jovanovich)

Film in Society, 1978 (Transaction)

Television as an Instrument of Terror, 1978 (Transaction)

Media Analysis Techniques, 1982 (Sage); 2nd edition, 1998 (Sage) (in Chinese, Korean, & Italian); 3rd edition, 2004 (Sage)

Signs in Contemporary Culture, 1984 (Longman); 2nd edition, 1998 (Sheffield); Indonesian edition, 2003

Television in Society, 1986 (Transaction)

Semiotics of Advertising, 1987 (Herodot)

Media USA, 1988 (Longman); 2nd edition, 1991 (Longman)

Seeing Is Believing: An Introduction to Visual Communication, 1989 (Mayfield); 3rd edition, 2008 (McGraw-Hill)

Political Culture and Public Opinion, 1989 (Transaction)

Agitpop: Political Culture and Communication Theory, 1989 (Transaction)

Scripts: Writing for Radio and Television, 1990 (Sage)

Media Research Techniques, 1991; 2nd edition, 1998 (Sage)

Reading Matter, 1992 (Transaction)

Popular Culture Genres, 1992 (Sage)

An Anatomy of Humor, 1993 (Transaction)

Blind Men & Elephants: Perspectives on Humor, 1995 (Transaction)

Cultural Criticism: A Primer of Key Concepts, 1995 (Sage)

Essentials of Mass Communication Theory, 1995 (Sage)

Manufacturing Desire: Media, Popular Culture & Everyday Life, 1996 (Transaction)

Narratives in Popular Culture, Media & Everyday Life, 1997 (Sage)

Bloom's Morning, 1997 (Westview/HarperCollins)

The Art of Comedy Writing, 1997 (Transaction)

Postmortem for a Postmodernist, 1997 (AltaMira)

The Postmodern Presence, 1998 (AltaMira); 2006 (Marjin Kiri)
Media & Communication Research Methods, 2000 (Sage)
Ads, Fads and Consumer Culture, 2000 (Rowman & Littlefield)
Jewish Jesters, 2001 (Hampton Press)
The Mass Comm Murders: Five Media Theorists Self-Destruct,
    2002 (Rowman & Littlefield)
The Agent in the Agency, 2003 (Hampton Press)
The Portable Postmodernist, 2003 (AltaMira)
*Durkheim Is Dead: Sherlock Holmes Is Introduced to Social
    Theory*, 2003 (AltaMira)
Media and Society, 2003 (Rowman & Littlefield)
Ocean Travel and Cruising, 2004 (Haworth Hospitality Press)
Deconstructing Travel: A Cultural Perspective, 2004 (AltaMira)
*Making Sense of Media: Key Texts in Media and Cultural
    Studies*, 2004 (Blackwell)
Shop Till You Drop: Perspectives on American Consumer Culture,
    2004 (Rowman & Littlefield)
Vietnam Tourism, 2005 (Haworth Hospitality Press)
Mistake in Identity: A Cultural Studies Murder Mystery, 2005
    (AltaMira)
50 Ways to Understand Communication, 2006 (Rowman &
    Littlefield)
Thailand Tourism, 2008 (Haworth Hospitality Press)
The Golden Triangle, 2008 (Transaction)
The Academic Writer's Toolkit: A User's Manual, 2008 (Left
    Coast Press)
What Objects Mean: An Introduction to Material Culture, 2009
    (Left Coast Press)
Bali Tourism, 2010 (Routledge)
Tourism in Japan: An Ethno-Semiotic Analysis (Channel View
    Publications)
The Cultural Theorist's Book of Quotations (Left Coast Press)

PART I

Semiotic Theory

CHAPTER 1

The Science of Signs

Everything we do sends messages about us in a variety of codes, semiologists contend. We are also on the receiving end of innumerable messages encoded in music, gestures, foods, rituals, books, movies, or advertisements. Yet we seldom realize that we have received such messages and would have trouble explaining the rules under which they operate.

Maya Pines, "How They Know What You Really Mean," *San Francisco Chronicle,* Oct. 13, 1982

The basic unit of semiotics is the *sign*, defined conceptually as something that stands for something else, and, more technically, as a spoken or written word, a drawn figure, or a material object unified in the mind with a particular cultural concept. The sign is this unity of word-object, known as a *signifier* with a corresponding, culturally prescribed content or meaning, known as a *signified*. Thus our minds attach the word "dog," or the drawn figure of a "dog," as a signifier to the idea of a "dog," that is, a domesticated canine species possessing certain behavioral characteristics. If we came from a culture that did not possess dogs in daily life, however

> unlikely, we would not know what the signifier "dog" means... When dealing with objects that are signifiers of certain concepts, cultural meanings, or ideologies of belief, we can consider them not only as "signs," but also as *sign vehicles*. Signifying objects carry meanings with them....
>
> Mark Gottdiener, *The Theming of America: Dreams, Visions, and Commercial Spaces*

The Greek root for semiology and for semiotics—the two terms used for the sciences that deal with signs—is *sēmeîon*, which means sign. These sciences have a long history, dating back more than two thousand years. The "father of medicine," Hippocrates (460–377 BC) was interested in signs and their relation to medical symptoms; philosophers and scholars after him, such as Plato, Aristotle, Saint Augustine, and Locke, also dealt with signs in their writings.

It is generally held that modern semiotics (the term now in favor) started with the work of two authors: Ferdinande de Saussure (1857–1913), a linguistics professor at the University of Geneva, who called his approach "semiology," and Charles S. Peirce (1839–1914), a philosopher at Harvard University, who called his science "semiotics."

Jonathan Culler, a biographer of Saussure, explains the importance of semiotics in his book *Ferdinand de Saussure* (1976:4):

> The notion that linguistics might be useful in studying other cultural phenomena is based on two fundamental insights: first, that social and cultural phenomena are not simply material objects or events but objects and events with meaning, and hence signs; and second, that they do not have essence but are defined by a network of relations.

These ideas have been enormously influential, and Saussure's book is now considered one of the most important works of the twentieth century. In this chapter I will provide an introduction to some of the more important concepts of semiotics so that you will be able to understand how semioticians arrive at their insights. For those interested in pursuing the subject further, I have listed a number of books in the bibliography on the subject. There are some fifty books on the subject available at Amazon.com and 560,000 websites found on Google that deal with semiotics.

The Semiotic Theories of Saussure and Peirce: An Overview

Saussure's book, *Course in General Linguistics*, published posthumously in 1915, is made of notes from his students that were collected and put together by Charles Bally and Albert Sechehaye. He offered an important insight into the roles of signs in society in his *Course in General Linguistics* when he wrote (1966:16):

> Language is a system of signs that expresses ideas, and is therefore comparable to a system of writing, the alphabet of deaf-mutes, symbolic rites, polite formulas, military signals, etc. But it is the most important of these systems.
>
> A science that studies the life of signs within society is conceivable; it would be part of social psychology and consequently of general psychology; I shall call it *semiology* (from Greek *sēmeîon* "sign"). Semiology would show what constitutes a sign, what laws govern them.

For Saussure signs have two parts: a sound-image or *signifier* and a concept or *signified*; it is crucially important to understand that the relation between the *signifier* and *signified* is not natural but arbitrary and based on convention. This means that the meaning of signs can change over time. According to him, signs can be studied two ways: synchronically, at a given

Ferdinand de Saussure

point in time, and diachronically, as they develop or evolve over time.

Saussure offered an important insight about concepts, based on the nature of language. Concepts, he explained, are defined differentially; that is, in terms of what they aren't. He explained that it is the relative position of signs in a statement that determines their meaning, not their intrinsic value. No sign, then, has meaning by itself, and its meaning is always a function of its relationship with other signs. What this means is that when we are dealing with concepts, because of the nature of language we tend to think in terms of polar oppositions such as cheap and expensive, rich and poor, happy and sad. Words are signs, and the meaning of a word depends upon the context in which it is found.

As Jonathan Culler explains in his book *Ferdinand de Saussure: Revised Edition* (1986:34):

The fact that these concepts, or signifieds, are arbitrary divisions of a continuum means that they are not autonomous entities, each of which is defined by some kind of essence.

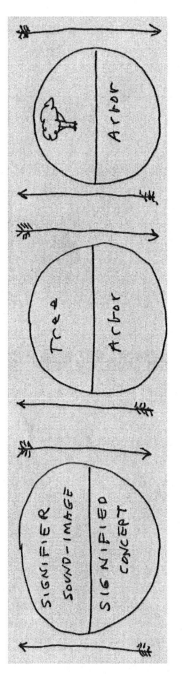

Tree arbor

They are members of a system and are defined by their relations to the other members of that system.

So there aren't any intrinsic links between signifiers and signifieds, and the meaning of signifieds or concepts is explained negatively and tied to their place in the system in which they are found.

Saussure explained why the mind tends to function in terms of contrasts and oppositions when he wrote that concepts are purely differential. It sounds like double-talk to say this, but what Saussure argues is that we only know what a concept means by knowing what is doesn't mean, and more particularly, by knowing its opposite. It is because of the nature of language that when it comes to concepts, our minds think in terms of oppositions. These oppositions have to be related or tied to something they have in common; for example, sexual orientation (gay or straight) or wealth (rich and poor).

That's why writers often use contrasts (oppositions) and comparisons to help clarify ideas. In Robert Jay Lifton's essay, "Who Is More Dry? Heroes of Japanese Youth," found in his book *History and Human Survival*, we see how contrasts and comparisons work (1974:104):

> In postwar Japan, especially among young people, it is good to be "dry" (or *durai*) rather than "wet" (or *wetto*). This means—in the original youth language, as expanded by the mass media—to be direct, logical, to the point, pragmatic, casual, self-interested, rather than polite, evasive, sentimental, nostalgic, dedicated to romantic causes, or bound by obligation in human relations; to break out of the world of cherry blossoms, haiku, and moon-viewing into a modern era of bright sunlight, jazz, and Hemingway (who may be said to have been the literary god of dryness). Intellectual youth, of course, disdain these oversimplified categories. But they too have made the words durai and *wetto* (typical examples of

Durai (Dry)	Wetto (Wet)
Young	Old
Direct	Evasive
Logical	Romantic causes
To the point	Polite
Pragmatic	Sentimental
Self-interested	Bound by obligations
Sunlight	Moon viewing
Hemingway	Haiku

Figure 1.1   Wet and Dry in Japan

postwar Japanized English) part of their everyday vocabulary, and they find dry objects of admiration in an interesting place: in American films about cowboys and gunmen.

Lifton analyzes the concept of "dryness" in Japanese culture and helps readers understand it by contrasting its opposite, "wetness."

In figure 1.1, which is based upon the material in the quotation above, we can elicit the oppositions in Lifton's text more clearly.

Saussure suggests that it is the nature of language that makes us use contrasts and comparisons, and this passage from Lifton is based on a set of oppositions he finds in Japanese culture. It is often a good idea to use charts and tables in situations where you wish to deal with complicated ideas and relationships. Quoting the text from Lifton and also offering the chart enables readers to Lifton's points see more clearly.

Peirce's approach to signs is different from Saussure's. He wrote that a sign "is something which stands to somebody for something in some respect or capacity" (*Collected Papers of Charles Sanders Peirce*, 1958) (quoted in Jay Zeman, "Peirce's Theory of Signs," in T. Sebeok, ed. *A Perfusion of Signs*, 1977, p. 24). He developed a typology that had three kinds of signs: *icons*, which signify by resemblance;

indexes, which signify by causal connections, and *symbols*, which signify by convention and have to be learned. As Peirce explained:

> Every sign is determined by its object, either first, by partaking of the characters of the object, when I call the sign an *Icon*; secondly, by being really and in its individual existence connected with the individual object, when I call the sign an *Index*; thirdly, by more or less approximate certainty that it will be interpreted as denoting the object, in consequence of a habit (which term I use as including a natural disposition), when I call the sign a *Symbol*. (Quoted in J. Jay Zeman, "Peirce's Theory of Signs," in T. Sebeok, *A Perfusion of Signs*, 1977:36)

Photographs, for example, are iconic; smoke that is generated by fire is indexical; and flags are symbolic. Many semioticians tend to combine both Saussurean semiology and Peircean semiotics in their work, especially in fields such as cultural studies.

C.S. Peirce

Many semioticians, generally in academic institutions, focus their attention on semiotic theory and the historical development of semiotics, but others are more interested in applying semiotics, often in combination with other theories, to culture and society. Semiotics is often used in conjunction with Marxist theory and psychoanalytic theory by scholars in culture studies. What semiotic theory offers is an explanation of how people find meaning in their everyday lives, in the media they consume, and the messages they receive from marketers and advertisers in contemporary commercial culture.

Some Contemporary Semiotic Theorists

Umberto Eco, an Italian semiotician and novelist and a professor of semiotics at the University of Bologna, explains in his book *A Theory of Semiotics* that signs are anything that can be used to substitute for something else. That something else doesn't have to exist or be somewhere, he adds, which means that semiotics studies anything that can be used to lie, for if something cannot be used to lie, Eco writes, it can't be used to tell the truth or communicate anything.

As Eco writes in *A Theory of Semiotics* (1976:7):

Semiotics is concerned with everything that can be taken as a sign. A sign is everything which can be taken as significantly substituting for something else. This something else does not necessarily have to exist or to actually be somewhere at the moment in which a sign stands for it. Thus semiotics is in principle the discipline studying everything which can be used in order to lie. If something cannot be used to tell a lie, conversely it cannot be used to tell the truth; it cannot in fact be used "to tell" at all. I think that the definition of a "theory of the lie" should be taken as a pretty comprehensive program for a general semiotics.

We may say that signs have a double valence and people can and often do lie with signs; for example, women and men with brown or black hair who dye their hair blonde or women and men who cross-dress. Eco would say that because we can "lie" with signs, we can use signs to find truths.

Marshall McLuhan (1911–1980) is not generally considered a semiotician but I would argue that his book *The Mechanical Bride: Folklore of Industrial Man*, written in 1951, is a semiotically informed study of American commercial culture, even though he didn't use the term "semiotics" in it. He writes in his preface that he wanted "to apply the method of art analysis to the critical evaluation of society" (1951:vi). In *The Mechanical Bride*, McLuhan discusses comic strips, the front pages of newspapers, and a number of advertisements for such products as RCA radios, GE lamps, Clark Grave Vaults, Thor Automatic Gladirons, Life Savers, the Mutual Benefit Life Insurance Company, and Squibb Cod Liver Oil. He deconstructs these advertisements and shows how advertisers sell products and services by manipulating people and capitalizing upon their basic values.

The French semiologist Roland Barthes (1915–1980) was one of the most important contemporary semioticians of consumer culture. His book, *Mythologies*, published in French in 1957 and in English in 1972, offered a semiotically informed dissection of French media and commercial culture. As he explained in the preface to the 1970 edition (1972:9),

> I had just read Saussure and as a result acquired the conviction that by treating "collective representations" as sign-systems, one might…account *in detail* for the mystification which transforms petit-bourgeois culture into a universal nature.

In *Mythologies,* Barthes offered a semiological/semiotic analysis of topics such as margarine, toys, soap powders and detergents, milk, wine, plastic, and the new Citroen. What Barthes did was to show how semiotics, in combination with Marxist theory, could explain how these products were being presented to the French public and the different mystifications and hidden ideologies found in these presentations. In the second half of the book he dealt with myth, including his discussion of myth as a semiological system. *Mythologies* is considered one of the classic examples of the semiotic analyses of consumer cultures. Barthes wrote another book, *Empire of Signs*, in which he used semiotics to analyze certain aspects of Japanese culture that interested him, and wrote many other books on a variety of subjects using semiotic theory.

An American semiotician, Marshall Blonsky, titled his book *American Mythologies*, which suggests that his book would do for American culture what Barthes' *Mythologies* did for France.

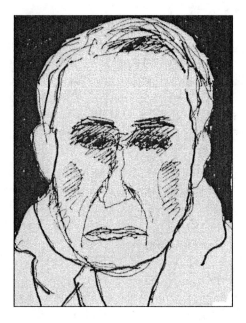

Roland Barthes

Blonsky's book is highly self-reflexive and autobiographical, but it does deal with certain aspects of consumer culture, such as clothing, food, automobiles, and advertising.

Symbols

Symbols are a complicated matter. Saussure believed that symbols are never completely arbitrary, suggesting that there is usually some kind of quasi-arbitrary or rudimentary bond between symbolic signifiers and what they signify. He uses the example of a symbol of justice, a pair of scales, and says this symbol cannot be replaced by any symbol, such as a chariot, and still convey its meaning. A more popular symbol of justice involves a blind goddess holding scales to signify impartiality. The problem is we have to learn to associate the scales with justice. Just seeing a set of scales or a blind goddess with scales does not automatically make us think of justice.

Semiotically speaking, symbols are things with important historical and cultural meanings, such as the cross for Christians, the Star of David for Jews, and the American flag for Americans. These symbols are tied to history and play important roles in every society. The anthropologist Clifford Geertz discussed symbols in his book *The Interpretation of Cultures* (1973:45):

Thinking consists not of "happenings in the head" (though happenings there and elsewhere are necessary for it to occur) but of a traffic in what have been called, by G. H. Mead and others—significant symbols—words for the most part but also gestures, drawings, musical sounds, mechanical devices like clocks, or natural objects like jewels—anything, in fact, that is disengaged from its mere actuality and used to impose meaning upon experience. From the point of view of any particular individual, such symbols are largely given. He finds them already current in the community in which is he is born and they remain, with some additions, subtractions, and partial alterations he may or may not have had a hand in, in circulation when he dies.

Geertz argued that we learn the meaning of symbols as we grow up in a certain culture or subculture and that the symbol's importance is enhanced by historical events and other happenings in that culture. Symbols help us make sense of things and play an important role in shaping our behavior in many areas: religion (the cross), nationalism (the flag), status (the kind of car we drive).

Denotation and Connotation

Semiotic theorists are interested in the difference between denotation and connotation. Denotation involves a literal and detailed description of the meaning of a word or the measurements of objects. Connotation, on the other hand, involves the cultural meanings and myths connected to words and to things. As Rosalind Coward and John Ellis explain in their book *Language and Materialism: Developments in Semiology and the Theory of the Subject* (1977:28):

> The mechanism of myth is the way that habitual representations tangle themselves up in everyday objects and practices so that these ideological meanings come to seem natural, the common-sense reality of that object or practice. There are therefore two systems of meaning: the denotative and the connotative, the "object language" (the film, the toy, the meal, the car inasmuch as they signify) and the myth which attaches itself to it, which takes advantage of the form of this denotative language to insinuate itself.

One of the most important insights semioticians offer us is that ideologies seek to present themselves and their theories as natural rather than historical, which means that since they are natural, and part of the scheme of things, they cannot be changed. If they were created by people they could be changed by them, as conditions changed.

Let us consider an important American cultural artifact— the Barbie˙ doll. From a denotation perspective, a Barbie doll is 11.5 inches tall, and has the following measurements: 5.25 inches by 3 inches by 4 inches. It was invented in 1959. This material is all factual and is denotation. The connotations of Barbie dolls are more complicated, for here we are dealing with what these dolls reflect about American culture and society and their symbolic and mythic significance. Sociologist Charles Winick, in his book *Desexualization in American Life*, provides a psychological and cultural interpretation of Barbie dolls and other similar dolls. He suggests that Barbie dolls reflect a basic change in manner in which the United States (and other countries where Barbie dolls are popular) deal with the way children are socialized. Little girls now learn how to become sexually attractive and practice having romantic relations with boys instead of rehearsing for motherhood by playing with baby dolls. They also learn how to be consumers. If Winick is right, Barbie dolls have changed the way little girls develop and have profoundly affected relationships, when the girls grow up, between men and women.

Metaphor and Metonymy

Technically speaking, metaphors are figures of language that communicate by analogy and use some form of the verb "to be"; that is, we understand what something is by comparing it to something else that is similar to it in certain respects. Thus, if we say "my love is a rose," we are comparing our loved one to a beautiful flower, a rose. There is a weaker form of metaphor called a simile, which uses "like" or "as" in its comparison.

Saying "my love is like a rose" is a simile, and isn't as strong a comparison.

Metaphor: My love *is* a rose
Simile: My love *is like* a rose

Metaphors, it turns out, are an important component of our thinking. As linguists George Lakoff and Mark Johnson write in their book *Metaphors We Live By* (1980:3):

Metaphor is for most people a device of the poetic imagination and the rhetorical flourish—a matter of extraordinary rather than ordinary language. Moreover, metaphor is typically viewed as a characteristic of language alone, a matter of words rather than thought or action. For this reason, most people think they can get along perfectly well without metaphor. We have found, on the contrary, that metaphor is pervasive in everyday life, not just in language but in thought and action. Our ordinary conceptual system, in terms of which we both think and act, is fundamentally metaphoric in nature. The concepts that govern our thought are not just matters of the intellect. They also govern our everyday functioning, down to the most mundane details. Our concepts structure what we perceive, how we get around in the world, and how we relate to other people. Our conceptual system thus plays a central role in defining our everyday realities. If we are right in suggesting that our conceptual system is largely metaphorical, what we experience and what we do every day is very much a matter of metaphor.

Metaphors, then, play an important role in determining the way we perceive the world and act in it because our concepts govern the way we behave.

We use metaphors because it is through analogies, including comparisons and contrasts, that we make sense of the world. If you are writing about something and can use a metaphor to help describe or explain it, you will be helping your readers by giving them an orientation that will help them better understand what you've written. Metaphors all have implications or what we might describe as "hidden imperatives" that come with them, even though we may not be aware of them.

For example, take the metaphor "Love is a game." That notion carries a number of implications about games that apply to love:

People cheat at games.
People get tired of playing games and they eventually end.
Games are not serious but diversions.
Games have rules.

You can see that if you accept the metaphor "Love is a game" as true, the logical implications of that notion are troubling.

In many cases, we use metaphors to provide information about something we don't know about. If a friend fixes you up with a blind date and you ask the friend what the woman he's fixed you up with looks like, he can provide some information to you by saying, "She looks a lot like Marilyn Monroe" or some other movie star or celebrity or person you know. If you want to know what goat meat tastes like, you can ask someone who has eaten goat and if he or she says "it tastes a lot like chicken," you have a pretty good idea of what goat meat tastes like.

The other important kind of figurative language is metonymy, which communicates by association. As we grow up and become imprinted with culture codes, we learn all kinds of associations, which means that metonymy can rely on information we already have in our heads (i.e., conventional associations) to convey information. For example, we know that people who own Rolls Royce automobiles are very rich, which means that when advertisers want to suggest a product is very upscale and high end, they often use Rolls Royces or other expensive automobiles to help people make the connections. I call this phenomenon "gilt by association."

There is a weaker form of metonymy called synecdoche, which uses a part to stand for a whole. For example, using the Pentagon to stand for the U.S. military or the American flag to stand for the United States of America is metonymic. Lakoff and Johnson explain the differences between metaphor and metonymy in *Metaphors We Live By* as follows (1980:36):

> Metaphor and metonymy are different *kinds* of processes. Metaphor is principally a way of conceiving of one thing in terms of another, and its primary function is understanding. Metonymy, on the other hand, has primarily a referential function, that is, allows us to use one entity to *stand for* another. But metonymy is not merely a referential device. It also serves the function of providing understanding.

We can see, then, that metaphor and metonymy are very important devices for helping us understand relationships among things, which means they also play an important role in shaping our thinking.

Because they provide shortcuts to generating information, advertisers use metaphor and metonymy a great deal. Metaphor allows advertisers to convey information very quickly, and metonymy allows advertisers to use information stored in our heads, in the form of codes, for their particular purposes. These kinds of figurative language can also be expressed in images in advertisements and commercials, which means they often have a powerful emotional impact on us.

Tony Schwartz, a media theorist, has argued that the standard "transportation" theory of media is inadequate and suggests a different one, which he calls the "responsive chord" theory. He writes in his book *Media: The Second God* (1983:24–25):

> Many of our experiences with electronic media are coded and stored in the same way they are perceived. Since they do not undergo a symbolic transformation, the original experience is more directly available to us when it is recalled.

Also, since the experience is not stored in a symbolic form, it cannot be retrieved by symbolic cues. It must be evoked by a stimulus that is coded the same way as the stored information is coded.

The critical task is to design our package of stimuli so that it resonates with information already stored within an individual and thereby induces the desired learning or behavioral effect. Resonance takes place when the stimuli put into our communication evoke *meaning* in a listener or viewer.

What this means is that advertisers can use the information stored in our heads for their purposes and don't have to convey information to us, just strike a chord that resonates with what we already know. It is a much quicker and much more effective process. As I suggested earlier, since everyone knows that Rolls Royces are very expensive cars, advertisers can use associations with these automobiles if they want to suggest that their product is "high quality" and the kind of product used by wealthy people who are "in the know" about what products are good. If an advertiser used a very expensive sports car like a Ferrari, it would convey different associations in the minds of audiences of advertisements than a Rolls Royce does.

Language and Speech

We must distinguish between language, which is a social institution that has rules about how words are to be used (found in dictionaries), and speech, which is the way individuals use language. Saussure explained the differences between language and speech in his *Course in General Linguistics* (1966:14):

Language is a well-defined object in the heterogeneous mass of speech facts. It can be localized in the limited segment of the speaking-circuit where an auditory image becomes associated with a concept. It is the social side of speech, outside the individual who can never create or modify it by himself; it exists only by virtue of a sort of contract signed by the members of the community. Moreover, the individual must always serve an apprenticeship in order to learn the functioning of a language; a child assimilates it only gradually.

We may say, then, that language is a social institution that expresses ideas by using signs, whose meanings are based on convention. As we grow up in any society, we learn and are taught the codes and rules that govern language use. If we do not abide by these rules, we will not speak or write the language correctly. But speech affects language, which explains why dictionaries are always being revised, to deal with new words that come into being through speech. Dictionaries, we must remember, record how language is used conventionally.

We can see the difference between language and speech in the world of fashion. Fashion—by which I mean the clothes we wear—is the equivalent of speech and represents all the clothes available to us, just as language represents all the words available to us, as found in dictionaries. What we choose to wear is the equivalent of speech. We may think of what we wear each day as the equivalent of a sentence, and of various rules about what goes with what as analogous to fashion codes.

The food we eat can also be considered the equivalent of speech and all the food that is available as the equivalent of language. There are certain codes we learn, as we grow up in various nationalities, ethnic groups, religious groups, and subcultures that involve the way we think about food. Observant Jews, for example, only eat Kosher beef and do not eat pork, shrimp, or lobster. They also do not have milk and meat at the same time, due to a prohibition against doing so in the Bible. Muslims do not eat pork due to a prohibition against it in their religious texts. So, gastronomically speaking, we find that we are at the Tower of Babel level and that people have many different kinds of speech reflected in their food choices, and these are based on codes we all learn as we grow up.

Language	Speech
Social institution	Personal choices
All foods available	What an individual eats
Dialects	Ethnic and national cuisines
Sentence	Each day's meals
Grammar	Culinary codes
Dictionaries	Cookbooks

Figure 1.2   Language and Speech as They Relate to Food

We can see the relationships between language and speech as they relate to food figure 1.2.

What is interesting to notice is that in many families nowadays, the meals that are served don't change that much from week to week, and people eat a rather limited number of foods on a weekly basis. We tend to eat the same things over and over again, which is analogous, when it comes to language, to saying the same things over and over again. At the same time, most families have a number of cookbooks, which contain thousands of recipes but only a few of which tend to be used. Many people, when they want to sample different foods, do so by going to ethnic restaurants, which explains why there are so many Chinese, Japanese, Thai, Vietnamese, Italian, and French restaurants in most cities and, in my case, within ten miles of where I live.

Saussure said that in language there are only differences. The same applies to foods, and for many people it is different national and ethnic cuisines that they desire when they go to restaurants. Unless there are unusual reasons, why should a family go out to eat if they're going to get the same food they have at home?

In his book *The Culture Code*, Clotaire Rapaille, who is from France, discusses the difference between American and French attitudes toward cheese. He writes (2006:25):

The French Code for cheese is ALIVE. This makes perfect sense when one considers how the French choose and store cheese. They go to a cheese shop and poke and prod the cheeses, smelling them to learn their ages. When they choose one they take it home and store it at room temperature in a cloche...The American code for cheese is DEAD. Again, this makes sense in context. Americans "kill" their cheese through pasteurization (unpasteurized cheeses are not allowed into this country), select hunks of cheese that have been prewrapped—mummified if you will—in plastic (like body bags), and store it, still wrapped airtight, in a morgue also known as a refrigerator.

This is not quite correct, for in gourmet stores and upscale markets, one can buy cheeses from America and all over the world that are "alive" and not wrapped in plastic, but most Americans don't buy these cheeses and instead store cheese in refrigerators. So culture codes tell us how to think about cheese and many other foods.

Codes

I have already mentioned codes and dealt with them in passing, but the subject demands more attention. What we call culture can be seen as a collection of codes that tell us what to eat, how to dress, and how to relate to others. As Rapaille mentioned above, notes, most of these codes are imprinted on children as they grow up in a family in a region of some country. Some codes are national, others are regional, and others stem from smaller entities such as parts of a city or a family's socioeconomic, ethnic, and religious identity.

Rapaille adds that "Once an imprint occurs, it strongly conditions our thought processes and shapes our future actions. Each imprint helps make us more of who we are. The combination of imprints defines us" (2006:6). Because we are exposed to codes at an early age—the process takes place until we are seven years old, Rapaille suggests—and either pick them up by osmosis or are learn them by observation, we internalize them and thus are unaware of the role they play in our lives. They seem to be a natural part of our experience, even though they are, in fact, socially constructed. If the codes we learn when we are children do, in fact, shape our behavior in profound ways, we can understand Freud's suggestion that "the child is the father of the man." He meant it psychologically, but we can also suggest it applies to our national cultures.

Rapaille mentions the goal he set for himself as a decoder of cultures. He writes (2006:9,10):

> If I could get to the source of these imprints—if I could some-how "decode" elements of culture to discover the emotions and meanings attached to them—I would learn a great deal about human behavior and how it varies across the planet. This set me on the course of my life's work. I went off in search of the Codes hidden within the unconscious of every culture.

Learning to understand culture codes, then, becomes a means of understanding human behavior, keeping in mind, Rapaille cautions, that although all human beings share certain needs, people in different countries are quite different, since they all have different imprintings and culture codes. There are, Rapaille suggests, three different kind of unconscious: the Freudian individual unconscious, the Jungian collective unconscious, and a cultural (by which he means national) unconscious, and they all shape our behavior. It is the national or cultural codes that interest Rapaille most, since his work involved figuring out how to market products to people in different countries.

Daniel Chandler, a British semiotician, deals with codes in his book *Semiotics: The Basics*. As he explains (2002:147–148):

> Since the meaning of a sign depends on the code within which it is situated, codes provide a framework within which

signs make sense. Indeed, we cannot grant something the status of a sign if it does not function within a code...The conventions of codes represent a social dimension in semiotics: a code is a set of practices familiar to users of the medium operating with a broad cultural framework. Indeed, as Stuart Hall puts it, "there is no intelligible discourse without the operation of a code..." Society itself depends on the existence of such signifying systems. When studying cultural practices, semioticians treat as signs any objects or actions which have meaning to the members of a cultural group, seeking to identify the rules or conventions of the codes which underlie the production of meaning within that culture.

This means that one of the main purposes of semiotics is to identify the hidden codes that shape our beliefs and the way we find meaning in the world. One of the most important things that semioticians do is to "decode" various aspects of a culture, whether it be signs found in advertisements, rituals, food practices, or fashion. Codes shape our behavior as individuals and as members of groups, societies, nations, and cultures.

Chandler suggests that there are three basic kinds of codes: social codes (involving language, our bodies, commodities we use, and our behavior), textual codes (involving scientific practices, aesthetics, genres, and the mass media), and interpretive codes (involving perception, aesthetics, and ideologies). In figure 1.3, drawn from his writing, we find correlations between his three kinds of codes and the kinds of knowledge required of semioticians.

The important thing to recognize about codes is that they pervade our lives; you can think of them as culturally specific rule books that we have internalized that tell us how to make sense of the world and how to behave in all the different situations in which we find ourselves. Codes affect everything from how we think about cheese, what we wear, what we find suitable for eating, how we relate to others, how we raise children, what gestures

Kind of Code	Knowledge Required
Social codes:	The world
Textual codes	Media and genres
Interpretive codes	The relationship between social and textual codes

Figure 1.3 Chandler on Kinds of Codes

we use, and how we look at other people, to how we are to be buried after we die.

As Chandler explains (2002:154):

> Within a culture, social differentiation is "over-determined" by a multitude of social codes. We communicate our social identities through the work we do, the way we talk, the clothes we wear, our hairstyles, our eating habits, our domestic environments and possessions, our use of leisure time, our modes of traveling and so on. Language is a key marker of social identity.

He mentions the work of the British sociologist Basil Bernstein, whose research suggested that there are differences between the way children in the working classes and middle classes speak in Britain. He called the working-class use of language a "restricted" code and the middle-class use of language an "elaborated" code.

We can see the difference between these two codes in figure 1.4, taken from Bernstein's writings but constructed by myself.

These codes are important because the codes the children learned played an important role in their future development and adult life. Bernstein's work suggests that the way we use language shapes our perception of the world, so in this context too, the codes functioned as a matrix through which the ideas and thoughts of the children were filtered. We also know that the accents people have give us impressions about them, and the way we think about a person from Britain who

Restricted Code	Elaborated Code
Working-class people	Middle-class people
Grammatically simple	Grammatically complex
Simple sentence structure	Complex sentence structure
Uniform vocabulary	Varied vocabulary
Few adjectives, adverbs	Many adjectives, adverbs
Low level of conceptualization	High level of conceptualization
Few qualifications used	Many qualifications used
Users unaware of code	Users aware of code

Figure 1.4 Basil Bernstein on Restricted and Elaborated Codes

uses the "received pronunciation" (found in royalty and the upper classes) usually differs considerably from someone with a Cockney accent.

Acura: An Example of Applied Semiotic Analysis

To see how semiotic codes affect consumer culture, let's take the case of the Acura motor car. Marcel Danesi, a prominent Canadian semiotician, discusses the naming of the Acura in his book *Understanding Media Semiotics*. He writes (2002:43):

A common strategy of the mass media is to build "coded meanings" into representations—i.e. to fashion something on the basis of some hidden code or codes. Take, as an example, the name "Acura" given to a Japanese automobile first built in the 1990s. This name has been fashioned, clearly, to be culturally ambiguous—it is imitative of both the structure of some Japanese words (such as *tempura*) and of most Italian words, which end typically in a vowel. This inbuilt ambiguity generates a system of connotations that are based on two sets of perceptions: (1) the popular view that Japanese technology and manufacturing is *accurate* and advanced; and (2) the common view of Italian as a language of "love," "poetry," and "song," and of Italians generally as "artistic," "romantic," and "friendly." These are the "coded meanings" that are built into the name "Acura." Like a recipe, the provide "hidden directions" for interpreting the name at a connotative level.

It would be interesting to know what the manufacturers of the automobile thought when they decided to name their car "Acura." Often products are named by companies that are paid huge amounts of money to think up names for automobiles and other products. I think it is a bit of a stretch to suggest that people who are thinking of buying an upscale car like the Acura resonate with the notion of accuracy in a car or that they connect it with Italian culture, since it ends in an "a." A lot of Japanese words also end with an "a" (such as "tempura"), and people purchasing the Acura generally know that it is manufactured by the Honda Motor Company and competes with other luxury automobiles such as the Toyota Lexus and various cars made by BMW and Mercedes Benz. But Danesi is correct in calling attention to the fact that a great deal of thinking goes into naming products and creating brands, and some people might see a connection between the name Acura and the word "accurate." We must also keep in mind, as I've pointed out a number of times in this discussion, that many of these processes operate at the unconscious level.

No Sign as a Sign

This process involves our not getting signs when we expect them, so no sign then becomes a sign. For example, if we are walking and come across someone we know and say "hello," but the person we greeted doesn't respond, that lack of response is a sign. We have to decide what it means. This process is important when we are dealing with expectations we have or with things that should happen but don't. Another example would be answering your phone, saying "hello," and not getting a response from anyone.

There is a famous Sherlock Holmes case that was solved because a dog didn't bark. A killer entered the grounds of an estate to murder someone but the dog guarding it didn't bark, which Holmes interpreted to mean that the dog knew the person and thus didn't bark.

We are led to conclude, then, that in some cases no sign functions as a sign—though we are often at a loss to interpret what the "no sign" response means. If we answer a phone and nobody responds, we tend to assume the person calling dialed the wrong number, but it could be a criminal planning to rob our house calling to see whether anyone is home or someone checking up on us for one reason or another. Not getting a "sign" when we expect one is generally disturbing. In our everyday interactions, not doing something expected of you is an example of "passive-aggressive" behavior, a form of aggression that involves not doing something you have been asked to do or are expected to do.

Signs within Signs

It is often the case that small signs are part of a larger sign system or collection of signs. Take the advertisement for Fidji perfume. In that advertisement, we find a number of important signs— what I call signemes. There is a snake coiled around a woman's neck, which from a Freudian perspective is a phallic symbol, and there is an orchid in the ear of the woman, flowers being symbols of women's genitals. And there are the words in the French language, which commonly is seen as being a signifier of sophistication. Most print advertisements contain a number of what I call signemes—small signs that are part of the larger sign system. It's interesting to know that in some countries this advertisement was run without the snake around the woman's neck.

Signs That Lie

I have already mentioned Umberto Eco's notion that semiotics is the science that deals with our ability to lie. He says that if something cannot be used to lie, it cannot be used to tell the truth. In our daily interactions, we often encounter people who are "lying" with signs, though in most cases we are unaware that this is occurring. If we see a blonde person with brown roots showing, we can be pretty confident that the "blonde" person is really a brunette. It has become stylish lately, for a reason that escapes me, for people to show the roots of their hair. It may be a way for "blondes" to acknowledge that they are playing with their identities by dyeing their hair. It is also possible to wear a wig and seem to be a blonde or redhead or have whatever hair color one wants.

There is a dilemma that women with dark hair who dye their hair blonde face. They are using their blonde hair to lie about their sexuality, for men have certain expectations about blondes—they are seen as "sexy" and "fun loving." Our attitudes about blondes are connected, it has been suggested, to atavistic attitudes about light and darkness. The work psychiatrist Roderick Gorney is relevant here. A review of his book *The Human Agenda* in *Newsweek* (June 12, 1972:100) explains:

> . . . he attempts to demonstrate a parallel between white man's worshipful attitude toward blondes and his racial fear and hatred of blacks. Do blondes really have more fun? "She is likely to find that she is expected not so much to *have* more fun as *be* more fun, particularly by men who want to exploit her for their own real, although more covert, adventures to the Fun ethic of childhood," Gorney writes. "A man will want her to have the 'innocent sweetness' of childhood, combined with a mature genital sexuality of which no child is capable." He thinks building a "self" based on this blond image party explains the tragedy of Marilyn Monroe.

We can see that lying with signs can have important consequences, not recognized by those who use signs to lie, even something as seemingly trivial as dyeing one's hair blonde.

Impersonators are people who appropriate someone else's identity by using that person's signs, as best they can. There are comedians who impersonate famous politicians and others, but their impersonations are overtly "lying" with signs, and the humor comes from the fact that a person seems so much like the person being impersonated. The most famous impersonation in recent years involve Tina Fey impersonating Sarah Palin, the Republican candidate for vice president. Fey brilliantly appropriated Palin's hairstyle, brand of eyeglasses, and way of talking as a means of ridiculing Palin. She often quoted Palin word for word, which added to the humor. Another form of impersonation is found in transvestites, who pretend to be members of a different gender. In some cultures, transvestites play an important role in the sex industry.

Imposters play different games. They generally appropriate professions by learning the jargon used in the profession and by faking credentials. There have been any number of imposters who pretended to be doctors and functioned for years, fooling real doctors by their brilliant acting. Some imposters are people of color who are light skinned enough to pass for white.

These examples suggest that a number of people lie with signs, and these lies vary from seemingly trivial "white lies" such as dyeing one's hair blonde to more serious lying about one's gender and race. The recent development of effective and easy-to-use hair straighteners means now that one of the former signifiers of being a black person—kinky hair—no longer is functional. In addition, many social scientists argue now that race is socially constructed, and as members of different races intermarry, the old signifiers of race—for whites and blacks and all people of color—are losing their importance and utility.

CHAPTER 2

Consumer Cultures

Consumerism has attached itself to a novel identity politics in which business itself plays in forging identities conducive to buying and selling. Identity here becomes a reflection of "lifestyles" that are closely associated with commercial brands and the products they label, as well as with attitudes and behaviors linked to where we shop, how we buy, and what we eat, wear, and consume. These attributes are in turn associated with income, class, and other economic forces that may appear to permit choice but are in fact largely overdetermined by demographics and socioeconomics and are beyond the control of individual consumers ... Branded lifestyles are not merely superficial veneers on deeper identities but have to some degree become substitute identities—forms of acquired character that have the potential to go all the way down to the core. They displace traditional ethnic and cultural traits and overwhelm the voluntary aspects of identity we choose for ourselves.

Benjamin Barber, *Consumed: How Markets
Corrupt Children, Infantilize Adults,
and Swallow Citizens Whole*

P eople need to eat, be clothed, and take care of other bio-logical imperatives, so consumption is a part of every-one's life in every society. But in some societies, generally in isolated agrarian ones, people live in what is essentially a subsistence economy, and consumption of material goods is not a major part of their lives. At the other extreme we have consumer cultures in which buying new products and ser-vices plays a major role in most everyone's lives, often to the detriment of public spending for roads, schools, medical care, and other similar public needs. The simplest way to define consumer cultures is that they are societies in which spend-ing for private "needs" and desires overwhelms spending on public ones.

Defining Consumer Cultures

Consumption is the flip side of production. In societies where you find mass production, you also find mass consumption, because somebody has to purchase the things that are made. In consumer cultures, people are taught, convinced—what you will—thanks to advertising and other cultural imperatives, to consume much more than they need, often going into debt to maintain their desired lifestyles.

A British social scientist, Mike Featherstone, wrote a book, *Consumer Cultures & Postmodernism,* in which he argues there are three components to consumer culture (1991:13):

First is the view that consumer culture is premised upon the expansion of capitalist commodity production which has given rise to a vast accumulation of material culture in the form of consumer goods and sites for purchase and consump-tion. This has resulted in the growing salience of leisure and consumption activities in contemporary Western societies which, although greeted as leading to a greater egalitarian-ism and individual freedom by some, is regarded by others as increasing the capacity for ideological manipulation and "seductive" containment of the population from some alternative set of "better" social relations. Second, there is the more strictly sociological view that the satisfaction derived from goods relates to their socially structured access in a zero sum game in which satisfaction and status depend upon displaying and sustaining differences within conditions of inflation. The focus here is upon the different ways in which people use goods in order to create social bonds or distinctions. Third, there is the question of the emotional pleasures of consumption, the dreams and desires which become celebrated in consumer cultural imagery and particular sites of consumption, which variously generate direct bodily excitement and aesthetic pleasure.

I will be dealing with a number of these topics in this book as I explore, from a semiotic perspective, the social and cultural aspects of consumption. Our personal purchases may be, or may seem to be, individual actions that we take, but these purchases are connected to any number of things relating to our social identities and our cultures. Personal consumption is, I argue, just the tip of the consumer culture iceberg.

One thing that those who own the means of production in consumer cultures have to do is change people's attitudes from ideas that focus on thrift and saving to ideas that focus on consumption. Edward Bernays, a prominent public relations expert, explained how people's minds can be changed. He writes (quoted in Stuart Ewen's *Captains of Consciousness: Advertising and the Social Roots of Consumer Culture*, 1976:83–84):

> If we understand the mechanism and motives of the group mind, it is not possible to control and regiment the masses according to our will without their knowing it....
>
> Mass psychology is as yet far from being an exact science and the mysteries of human motivations are by no means all revealed. But at least theory and practice have combined with sufficient success to permit us to know that in certain

cases we can effect some change in public opinion...by operating a certain mechanism.

The argument Bernays makes is worth considering. Does public relations (and advertising) have the ability to shape a society's collective consciousness without anyone in that society recognizing what has happened? The implications are scary, but there seems to be evidence that at least in certain areas, involving purchases of products and goods, something similar to what Bernays is writing about has taken place. But there's more to the development of consumer cultures than advertising and other ways of shaping public opinion and desire.

The Sacred Origin of Consumer Cultures

In order for consumer cultures to develop, people have to change their mindsets and the way they think about consumption. One of the main things consumer cultures need to do, in order to develop, is to encourage people to cast off medieval notions about asceticism and minimizing consumption. It was the theologian, John Calvin (1509–1564), who attacked asceticism, which at the time was associated with Catholic thought, in his writings. Calvin argued (quoted in Van Tassel and McAharen, 1969:11–12)

> If we are only to pass through the earth, we ought undoubtedly to make such a use of its blessings as will rather assist than retard us in our journey. It is not without reason, therefore, that Paul advises us to use the world as though we used it not, and to buy with the same disposition with which we sell (I Cor. Vii:30,31). But as this is a difficult subject, and there is danger of falling into one of two opposite errors, let us endeavor to proceed on safe ground, that we may avoid both extremes.

Calvin argued that we must avoid two extremes: first, extravagant excesses and intemperance, and second, life-denying austerity and asceticism.

Calvin adds that those who have wealth and material goods should be seen as fulfilling God's desires (Van Tassel and McAharen, 1969:12–13)

> It must be laid down as a principle, that the use of the gifts of God is not erroneous when it is directed to the same end for which the Creator himself has created and appointed them for us; since he has created them for our benefit, not for our injury. . . . Now, if we consider to what end he has created the various kinds of aliment, we shall find that he intended to provide not only for our necessity, but likewise for our pleasure and delight. So in clothing, he has had in view not mere necessity, but propriety and decency. In herbs, trees, and fruits, besides their various uses, his design has been to gratify us by graceful forms and pleasant odors.

Living an ascetic life, Calvin suggests, "malignantly deprives us of the lawful enjoyment of the Divine beneficence, but which cannot be embraced 'til it has despoiled man of all his senses, and reduced him to a senseless block" (Van Tassel and McAharen, 1969:13). Calvin adds that we must differentiate between an ascetic extreme and its opposite, a life of gluttony and excess. The ascetic extreme focuses on abstinence and is too reductionistic, reducing life to its necessities while its opposite, gluttonous eating and drinking, distracts people from their most important task—the need to focus upon their spiritual life. As Calvin explains, "fastidiousness in our furniture, our habitations, and our apparel" as well as similar kinds of behavior distracts people from their most important duty—the need to look after their souls.

Calvin's ideas were discussed in the work of the German sociologist, Max Weber, whose book *The Protestant Ethic and the Spirit of Capitalism* offers a penetrating examination of the impact of the Protestant ethic on the development of capitalism in modern societies. Long before advertisers began trying to manipulate people,

Protestant theology, as espoused by Calvin, began to dissuade people from the value of asceticism and poverty and convince them that God wanted people to enjoy life and that consumption was divinely inspired.

Calvin espoused a different kind of asceticism from that promulgated by medieval Catholic theology. Calvin glorified hard work and using time profitably, so people could earn money and thus be able to consume as God wanted them to do. According to Weber, Calvinist theology led to providing a hardworking and diligent workforce, who believed that their place in society and in the scheme of things was determined by God and was a matter of divine providence. Weber described this thinking as follows (1958:177):

> The power of religious asceticism provided him [the bourgeois business man]...with sober, conscientious, and unusually industrious workmen, who clung to their work as to a life purpose willed by God. Finally, it gave him the comforting assurance that the unequal distribution of the goods of this world was a special dispensation of Divine Providence, which in these differences, as in particular grace, and pursued secret ends unknown to men.

Calvin explained that the unequal distribution of wealth is a result of "Divine Providence," which provides great comfort to wealthy people since this view justifies their status. This theory argues that efforts to ameliorate the lives of the poor are fruitless, for they go against Divine Providence. This notion, that people who are wealthy "deserve" to be so because their wealth is divinely inspired, still has many adherents today.

Weber also discusses the ideas of a Puritan minister, Richard Baxter, who believed that (1958:177) "the care for external goods should only lie on the shoulders of the 'saint like a light cloak, which can be thrown aside at any moment.' But fate decreed that the cloak should become an iron cage." What has happened, Weber suggests, is that our passion for material goods now dominates us, and is reflected in our cultures and the development of our national character. He writes (1958:182):

> No one knows who will live in this cage in the future, or whether at the end of this tremendous development entirely new prophets will arise, or there will be a mechanized petrification, embellished with a sort of convulsive self-importance. For of the last state of this cultural development, it might be truly said: "Specialists without spirit, sensualists without heart; this nullity imagines that it has attained a level of civilization never before achieved."

Weber's study of Calvin suggests is that there is an important, though generally unrecognized, religious or sacred dimension to our passion for consumption. He argues that the same passions and fervor that animate religious belief in people take on a secularized form and shape their behavior as consumers in contemporary societies. Adopting a religious perspective on things, we can say that shopping becomes, in an unconscious way and a disguised form, a sacred act. "Retail therapy" becomes not only something explained by Freud but also by religious thought. This passion we have for consumption, Calvin wrote, does not lie like a light cloak upon our shoulders but has wrapped itself around us, covering us completely— and taken control of us.

It was in the United States, Weber suggested, that the pursuit of wealth and the passion for consumption reached its zenith. The crash of American and worldwide consumer cultures that took place in the fall of 2008 suggests that consumer cultures, if they are not regulated and contained, have implicit self-destructive forces in them that eventually lead to terrible social and economic dislocations, trauma, and pain. This crash had a profound impact upon the way Americans related to consumer culture and felt about going into debt to buy things.

Psychological Imperatives in Consumer Cultures

We have seen how the Protestant ethic laid the theological roots that led to the development of contemporary consumer cultures. There is another aspect to the phenomenon that is worth considering: the psychological imperatives found in consumer cultures. In a classic work of psychoanalytic theory, Melanie Klein and Joan Riviere's *Love, Hate and Reparation,* Joan Riviere offers an overview of the mechanisms found in people. She writes, in a chapter titled "Hate, Greed and Aggression" (1937:4):

> The fundamental aim in life is to live and to live pleasurably. In order to achieve this, each of us tries to deal with and dispose of destructive forces in himself, venting, diverting and fusing them in such a way as to obtain the maximum *security* he can in life—and pleasures to boot—an aim which we achieve by infinitely various, subtle and complicated adaptations.

She adds that the outcomes in individuals are the result of two factors: the strength of the love and hate tendencies in each of us and the influence of our environments and society.

After making this point, Riviere considers various psychological phenomena such as aggression, projection, depreciation, envy, and greed. It is in her discussion of greed that she offers an explanation of the psychological impulses that lead to the desire for possessions and that collectively generate consumer cultures. She writes (1937:26–27):

> Some measure of greed exists unconsciously in everyone. It represents an aspect of the desire to live, one which mingled and fused at the outset of life with the impulse to turn aggression and destructiveness outside ourselves against others . . . By its very nature it is endless and never assuaged; and being a form of the impulse to live, it ceases only with death. The longing or greed for good things can relate to any and every imaginable kind of good—material possessions, bodily or

mental gifts, advantages and privileges; but, beside the actual gratification they may bring, in the depths of our minds they all ultimately signify one thing. They stand as proofs to us, if we get them, that we are ourselves good, and full of good, and so are worthy of love, or respect and honour, in return. Thus they serve as proofs and insurances against our fears of the emptiness inside ourselves, or of our evil impulses which make us feel bad...One great reason why a *loss* of any kind can be so painful is that unconsciously it represents the converse idea, that we are being exposed as *unworthy* of good things, and so our deepest fears are realized.

From a psychoanalytic standpoint, then, each of us has an unconscious need for material things, and the financial and psychological benefits that lead to our getting and having things can never be satisfied. We are, so to speak, hardwired to want things endlessly, since having things is an instinctive need we have to feel alive and good.

Riviere's analysis reminds us of Calvin's notions about material wealth as being divinely inspired and predestined and thus not capable of being changed by human institutions. This need to have good things, to take good things "into" us, is similar, in nature, to the mental process known as introjection. It is the opposite of projection, which involves expelling feelings of anger and hate, whatever we feel as bad and harmful, onto others. The degree to which we feel the need to have more and more things is connected to the societies into which we are born and raised. Greed, as Riviere explains it, is exacerbated in consumer cultures; people are under constant pressure from the values permeating their societies and the institutions functioning in them, such as advertising.

On the personal front, during a recent visit, my six-year-old grandson described himself as "greedy" and said that he should be given every toy or anything else he wanted. This is connected with his growing up in a society in which many children are taught to feel entitled to everything. An article in the October 21, 2008 issue of the *Wall Street Journal*, "The 'Trophy Kids' Go to Work" (based on Ron Alsop, *The Trophy Kids Grow Up: How the Millenial Generation is Shaking Up the Workplace"*) is relevant here. Alsop deals with the so-called "Millenial Generation," children born between 1980 and 2001, who have an inflated sense of entitlement, in part because of the way schools and parents have indulged them. They were babied and catered to, since parents and teachers feared injuring their "self-esteem." As a result, these "trophy kids" have an inflated notion about their abilities, feel they are superior to others, and harbor outlandish expectations as far as what they expect when they go to work.

The irony, Alsop writes, is that the managers who have to deal with the "trophy kids" now are the ones who, as parents, helped create them. Whether Alsop is correct in his analysis of the development of the Millenials and their impact is debatable. He suggests that the Millenials "want to be CEO tomorrow" but a number of years ago, when I did research on department stores, the managers of the stores told me the same thing. "We can't get secretaries," one of them told me. "They all want to start with my job." So although the Millenials probably do have an inflated sense of their superiority and their abilities, they don't seem to be too much different from the way young people behaved in previous generations.

Marxist Theory and Consumer Cultures

If the psychoanalytic perspective on consumer culture locates the driving force behind our desire to acquire goods in the human psyche and our need to feel good about ourselves, the Marxist perspective takes a different approach. For Marx, it is not consciousness that determines society but society that determines consciousness. As he writes in his *Preface to a Contribution to the Critique of Political Economy* (1964:51)

> In the social production which men carry on they enter into definite relations that are indispensable and independent of their will; these relations of production correspond to a definite

state of development of their material powers of production. The totality of these relations of production constitutes the economic structure of society—the real foundation, on which legal and political superstructures arise and to which definite forms of social consciousness correspond. The mode of production of material life determines the general character of the social, political and spiritual processes of life. It is not the consciousness of men that determines their being, but, on the contrary, their social being determines their consciousness.

The economic relationships found in a society become the "determinant element" in our thoughts. Beneath the superficial randomness of things, then, we find a kind of inner logic at work. The economic system of a society, what Marx called the "base," shapes the "superstructure," the ideas people have, ideas that are instrumental in determining the kinds of social, political, and economic arrangements they will make with one another and the institutions they will establish.

If social being determines consciousness, then, Marxist theory suggests, the roots of our consumer lust lie in the societies in which we live. As Marx writes (quoted in Fromm, 1962:50):

Every man speculates upon creating a new *need* in another in order to force him to a new sacrifice, to place him in a new dependency, and to entice him into a new kind of pleasure and thereby into economic ruin. Everyone tries to establish over others an *alien* power in order to find there the satisfaction of his own egoistic need.

For Marx, then, those who are in the ruling class and who own the means of production strive to create new "needs" and alien needs in people so as to maintain the class divisions in society. For Marxists, consumer cultures are the way the ruling classes divert the proletariat (the masses) and prevent them from developing a class consciousness and from thinking about political change and revolution.

There is, for Marxists, a connection between alienation and consumer culture. The term "alienation" means, literally, no ties and no connections, and for Marx it was one of the main problems found in capitalist societies. In these societies, workers are estranged and separated from their true interests and work only to earn money, which will then enable them to participate in consumption. As Marx explains (1964:169–170):

> The worker...feels himself at home only during his leisure, whereas at work he feels homeless. His work is not voluntary but imposed, *forced labour.* It is not the satisfaction of a need, but only a *means* for satisfying other needs. Its alien character is clearly shown by the fact that as soon as there is no physical or other compulsion it is avoided like the plague...The *alienation* of the worker in his product means not only that his labour becomes an object, takes on its own existence, but that it exists outside him, independently, and alien to him, and that it stands opposed to him as an autonomous power. The life which he has given to the objects sets itself against him as an alien and hostile force.

What happens, then, is that people become estranged, not only from their work, but also from their friends, from themselves, and from their lives. People become more and more alienated, becoming, finally, prisoners of their alienated needs and, Marx writes, "*self-conscious* and *self-acting*" commodities. But it isn't only the workers who are alienated in capitalist societies. For Marx, everyone in capitalist societies is alienated, for those who are members of the ruling classes are also alienated and always worried about political changes that might impinge on their domination.

It is alienation, Marxists argue, that leads people into consumer culture, for it is only when they purchase things that they find momentary gratification and escape from the alienation that plagues them. There is a vicious cycle at work here. Workers

Karl Marx

in capitalist countries feel alienated, and the more they work the more alienated they feel. They escape from this feeling of alienation by buying things and participating in consumer culture; but this costs money, so ironically they are forced to work harder and harder to escape from the effects of their work.

Advertising is the lubricant that helps the consumer society run, so for Marxists advertising is an institution of major importance. Advertising may sell products, but at the same time it sells the capitalist social order that makes it possible for workers to participate in consumer cultures. Advertising works by generating dissatisfactions and anxieties in people and feeds on the alienation that pervades capitalist societies. It assuages these feelings by focusing attention on private consumption. Thus people are led away from paying attention to the way the ruling classes dominate capitalist societies and the grossly unequal distribution of wealth found in them. Another thing advertising does is promote narcissism; it leads people to focus on their own personal wants or desires and to neglect social and political matters and the needs of others. In consumer societies it is private consumption that dominates, not expenditures for the good of the community.

Jean Baudrillard on Advertising and Consumer Cultures

Jean Baudrillard (1929–2007) was one of the most important French social scientists of the twentieth century. He devotes the last part of his book *The System of Objects* to advertising, because of its importance in consumer cultures. The book was published in French in 1968 and translated by James Benedict and published in English in 1996. It combines semiotics, Freudian psychoanalytic theory, and Marxism in a unique blend.

As Baudrillard explains (1996:164):

> Any analysis of the system of objects must ultimately imply an analysis of discourse *about* objects—that is to say, an analysis of promotional "messages" (comprising image and discourse). For advertising is not simply an adjunct to the system of objects; it cannot be detached therefrom, nor can it be restricted to its "proper" function (there is no such thing as advertising strictly confined to the supplying of information). This lack of proportion is the "functional" apotheosis of the system. Advertising in its entirety contributes a useless and unnecessary universe. It is pure connotation. It contributes nothing to production or to the direct practical application of things, yet it plays an integral part in the system of objects not merely because it relates to consumption but also because it itself becomes an object to be consumed.

Thus advertising sells consumption and is itself an object of consumption. His notion that advertising is pure connotation is a bit exaggerated, for some advertising is factual and functions as denotation, but mostly advertising is connotation. He adds that advertising faces a dilemma: There is so much advertising that the messages tend to cancel out each other, and claims by advertisers give way to counterclaims, leading to the problem of clutter—a problem that advertising agencies continually have to face.

But these claims, Baudrillard argues, are not what is crucial. We must understand that what is most important is that advertising offers a "leitmotiv" of needs (more precisely, wants) and gratifications. People don't believe in advertising, he argues, in the same way that they don't believe in Santa Claus, but they are affected by advertising's general thrust toward regression and infantilization and its ability to tell people of their hidden desires and finding ways to satisfy them.

Greg Rowland, in a personal communication, points out that more advanced advertising cultures have "developed connotative differentiation—emotional cues dominating messages in a way that would only have been seen in fine fragrance advertising... This is particularly true in soft-selling Britain where a near absence of rational claim is often a norm, even in laundry powder or automotive categories." This insight might explain why we are beginning to see advertising in the United States that doesn't seem to be pitching the product. The aim of this advertising, it would seem, is to plant emotional cues in us that can eventually be utilized to sell a product.

David F. Walsh, a sociologist at Goldsmiths, University of London, offers an overview of Baudrillard's theories. He discusses Baudrillard's combination of postmodern theory as it relates to consumer cultures and writes (in Chris Jenks, Ed., *Core Sociological Dichotomies*, 1998:30):

> For Baudrillard, contemporary society is a postmodern society which is no longer structured by production in which the individual conforms to its needs but by symbolic exchange. It is a heterogeneous society of different groups with their own codes and practices of everyday life at the level of discourse, lifestyles, bodies, sexuality, communication, etc. and it involves the rejection of the logic of production and its instrumental rationality that dominated the modernist society of

capitalism. Capitalism now has been replaced by a consumer society which is characterized by a proliferation of signs, the media and messages, environmental design, cybernetic steering systems, contemporary art and a sign culture. It is a society of simulations based on the new forms of technology and culture. Signs now take on a life of their own and come to be the primary determinants of social experience. Signs and codes replace reality and the world is experienced through images (simulation) to the point where the real as something different from the image disappears. A world of hyper-reality is created in which everything in the world is simulated in the sense that models created by images replace the real.

For Baudrillard, it is the cultural shock generated by postmodernism that explains the way contemporary societies function. Postmodernist theorists argue that around the 1960s, there was a fundamental rupture in our thinking, a major change in the

Jean Baudrillard

way people saw the world, and the old systems of thought that guided people, based on metanarratives (large, all-encompassing systems of thought found in religions, philosophy, and social theory) were abandoned.

One of the most celebrated explanations of postmodernism comes from the French scholar Jean-François Lyotard. In his book *The Postmodern Condition: A Report on Knowledge,* he writes (1984:xxiv):

> Simplifying to the extreme, I define *postmodern* as incredulity toward metanarratives. This incredulity is undoubtedly a product of progress in the sciences: but that progress in turn presupposes it. To the obsolescence of the metanarrative apparatus of legitimation corresponds, most notably, the crisis of metaphysical philosophy and of the university institution which in the past relied on it. The narrative function is losing its functors, its great hero, its great dangers, its great voyages, its great goal.

J-F Lyotard

This statement, in which Lyotard explains that postmodernism involves "incredulity toward metanarratives," is quite likely one of the most widely quoted definitions of the term ever written. Lyotard explains that we no longer have faith in wide-ranging, metanarratives (i.e., supernarratives)—the systems of belief and thought (as expounded in religions, political ideologies, and philosophy)—that we used in the past.

Now, in a postmodern world, we have a number of smaller and different narratives vying for our attention, leading to a crisis of legitimation. We don't know who has the right answers about important social and political questions, whose beliefs are correct, and what the difference is between right and wrong. In a postmodern world these questions are the subject of disputes. Is postmodernism relativistic? This is a debatable matter, one that is part of the controversy about postmodernism. Although postmodernists don't believe in any metanarratives, it doesn't mean they don't believe in any narratives. But how do we decide which narratives are correct?

In postmodernist societies, signs are all-important, and for Baudrillard they create a "hyper-reality" that seems more real than actual reality. The simulations now seem more real than the things they simulate, and underlying it all is the development of consumer cultures; for postmodern societies are, above all, consumer-crazed societies. In these societies, the things we purchase are no longer evaluated in terms of their use or functionality but rather in terms of what they signify about us—what they reveal about us, such as our taste, our style, our socioeconomic level, and our attitudes toward authority. This means that it is their semiotic meaning that is now all-important.

Ultimately, we find ourselves needing to consume endlessly; if we don't, we fear that we are not taking care of our needs. Baudrillard discusses this matter in his book *The Consumer Society: Myths and Structures,* which originally appeared in 1970 in French and 1998 in an English translation. His analysis indicates the pressures people feel in consumer societies (1998:80):

> Modern man spends less and less of his life in production within work and more and more of it in the *production* and continual innovation of his own needs and well-being. He must constantly see to it that all his potentialities, all his consumer capacities are mobilized. If he forgets to do so, he will be gently and insistently reminded that he has no right not to be happy. It is not, then, true that he is passive. He is engaged in—has to engage in—continual activity. If not, he would run the risk of being content with what he has and becoming asocial.
>
> Hence the revival of a *universal curiosity*...in respect to cookery, culture, science, religion, sexuality, etc. "Try Jesus" runs an American slogan. You have to try *everything*, for consumerist man is haunted by the fear of "missing" something, some form of enjoyment or other...It is no longer desire, or even "taste," or a specific inclination that are at stake, but a generalized curiosity, driven by a vague sense of unease—it is the "fun morality" or the imperative to enjoy yourself, to exploit to the full one's potential for thrills, pleasure or gratification.

The picture Baudrillard paints of people driven by hidden imperatives to enjoy themselves suggests that there is something destructive operating in consumer cultures and that people find themselves stressed and pressed to experience everything and miss nothing that will create pleasure. It is the same kind of fervor found in earlier times about religion and salvation that has been transformed and secularized into a passion for pleasure and a fear of not having the "right" things and missing any gratifications.

We can make a distinction between needs and desires. Our needs are relatively limited: We need food, housing, clothing, medical care, and not too many other things. Our desires, on the other hand, are limitless, infinite, and insatiable. It is the job of advertisers and marketers to find ways of manufacturing desire and of translating things we desire into things we feel we need. One way this is done is by fashion, by which I mean new products that are created to assuage our desire for differentiation and change. Fashion is, sociologically speaking, an institution, a structure found in society that continually introduces new products and changes the styling of products we already have.

Think, for example, of the evolution of MP3 players and of the spread of the iconic iPod and various competitors of the iPod. Every year new kinds of MP3 players are manufactured and new versions of previous MP3 players are created. Another good example would be software, new versions of which are being created all the time.

Fashion helps create a sense of dissatisfaction with what we already have and a desire for new products. Sometimes things wear out—like running shoes or articles of clothing. But generally we purchase new things because we've been led to feel that doing so will enhance our well-being. Most of us don't really need half the things we purchase, but we find ourselves wanting new products because we've been led to feel the things we already have are dull and no longer fashionable.

Thus, fashion as "constant change" is useful to manufacturers, who create new and revised versions of products and to individuals, for it enables them to purchase new products that enhances their sense of well-being and helps them differentiate themselves—through the sign value of the new purchases—from others. That is what Veblen dealt with in his theory of conspicuous consumption and what motivates our desire for "status symbols."

John Berger, a British Marxist, makes a point that is relevant here. In his book *Ways of Seeing,* he explains how advertising, which he calls publicity, works (1972:131, 132):

> It purposes to each of us that we transform ourselves, or our lives, by buying something more.

This more, it proposes, will make us in some way richer—even though we will be poorer for having spent our money.

Publicity persuades us of such a transformation by showing us people who have apparently been transformed and are, as a result, enviable. The state of being envied is what constitutes glamour. And publicity is the process of manufacturing glamour...Publicity is never a celebration of pleasure-in-itself. Publicity is always about the future buyer. It offers him an image of himself made glamorous by the product or opportunity it is trying to sell. The image then makes him envious of himself as he might be. Yet what makes this self-which-he-might-be enviable? The envy of others. Publicity is about social relations, not objects.

We are back, then, where we started, when I discussed Joan Riviere's Freudian psychoanalytic approach toward consumption, which is based on envy. What John Berger does is show how we are taught to be envious of ourselves, as we might or will be if we buy certain products or services, and that in our future state, when we have made these purchases, we will be envied by others. And that is because of the sign value of products, not their intrinsic value or the needs or desires that they satisfy.

Robert Coen, the leading authority on advertising expenditures, estimates that in 2007 we spent around $630 billion worldwide for advertising. In 2007 we spent about $280 billion on advertising in the United States. If you take the $630 billion spent worldwide for advertising and subtract the amount of money spent on advertising in the United States from that figure, you arrive at a figure for worldwide expenditures for advertising of about $350 billion (figure 2.1).

There are approximately 6.6 billion people in the world. When you subtract the 300 million people in the United States from this figure, you get 6.3 billion people outside of the United States who are exposed to $350 billion worth of advertising. These statistics can be somewhat misleading, for there are parts of the world where

	United States	**Rest of World**
Population	$300 million	$6.3 billion
Advertising	$280 billion	$350 billion

Figure 2.1 Global Advertising Expenditures

there is hardly any advertising and other parts, especially in first world countries, where there is a great deal—but most countries still have relatively little exposure compared to the United States.

These figures show people in the United States have to endure about twenty times as much advertising as people in other countries. A considerable percentage of our exposure to advertising takes the form of television commercials. A typical thirty-minute television show in the United States has seven minutes of commercials. Since we watch an average of four hours of television (per person) in the United States, we watch approximately an hour of commercials every day or around 365 hours of commercials a year.

To understand what this figure means, remember that a typical course in a university has forty classroom hours. This means that when Americans watch commercial television, their yearly "instruction" from television commercials is equivalent to about a year of college instruction—that is, taking nine university courses.

CHAPTER 3

Marketing Theory and Semiotics

Rather than unreflexively adopting a lifestyle, through tradition or habit, the new heroes of consumer culture make lifestyle a life project and display their individuality and sense of style in the particularity of the assemblage of goods, clothes, practices, experiences, appearance and bodily dispositions they design together into a lifestyle. The modern individual within consumer culture is made conscious that he speaks not only with his clothes, but with his home, furnishings, decoration, car and other activities which are to be read and classified in terms of the presence and absence of taste.

Mike Featherstone, *Consumer Culture &*
Postmodernism

Today's marketing isn't simply a business function. It's a philosophy, a way of thinking and a way of structuring your business and your mind. Marketing is more than a new ad campaign or this month's promotion. Marketing is part of everyone's job, from the receptionist to the board of directors. The task of marketing is never to fool the customer or endanger the company's image. Marketing's task is to design a product-service combination that provides real value to targeted customers, motivates purchase, and fulfills genuine customer needs.

Philip Kotler, John Bowen, James Makens,
*Marketing for Hospitality and
Tourism* (2nd edition)

W e have discussed semiotic theory in the first chapter and consumer cultures in the second chapter. In this chapter, we will turn our attention to marketing theory—the ideas, tactics, and strategies developed by marketers to be used to sell products and services and to meet the needs, desires, or wants people have.

Ernest Dichter and Motivation Research

Although each of us is different from everyone else, and we each have distinctive ideas, personalities, and systems of beliefs, for marketers, individuals aren't important. Marketing professionals have developed a number of different typologies by which they classify people, based on the notion that people in any particular classification group have certain things in common as far as their consumption practices are concerned. The examples I will deal with range from human beings everywhere to nationalities and to microgroups within a country.

I will begin with the work of Ernest Dichter, the "father" of motivation research, who was interested in what motivated people in general, though much of his work applied to people in the United States. Dichter developed a research methodology known as nondirective depth interviews. Using this method of interviewing people—he avoided asking people direct and often superficial questions about their choice of products—he used psychoanalytic theory and depth interviewing to find out what people unconsciously felt about various products and services. That is, he made use of psychoanalytic theory not to deal with neuroses, personality problems, and relationship difficulties of individuals, but to discover unconsciously held attitudes and beliefs in people that helped him understand the subject of interest to him: the mysterious matter of why consumers act the way they do.

As Dichter explained in *The Strategy of Desire* (1960:12):

> Whatever you attitude toward modern psychology of psychoanalysis, it has been proved beyond any doubt that many of our daily decisions are governed by motivations over which we have no control and of which we are often quite unaware.

This means that our motivations are, in Freudian terms, buried in the unconscious elements of our psyches, that we are unaware of them, and, as Freud explained, we resist becoming aware of them. Freud's topographic hypothesis divided the human psyche into three discrete parts:

consciousness, or that which we are aware of;

a *pre-conscious* (material buried just beneath our consciousness that can be recalled); and

the *unconscious* (material buried in our psyches and unavailable to us, but accessible to trained experts through depth interviewing and dream analysis.

An iceberg (figure 3.1) is an excellent visual metaphor for these three levels of the psyche.

The area of our psyches of which we are conscious is the part of the iceberg floating above the water, the part that we can see. It is a very small percentage of the iceberg, which extends deep into the water. There is a thin layer of the iceberg just beneath the surface, perhaps five or six feet, that we can dimly perceive, which represents what Freud called the pre-conscious part of our psyches. And buried in the darkness, hidden from the sun (and our consciousness) is the unconscious, which constitutes most of the human psyche. What psychoanalytic theory tells us is that the unconscious part of the psyche frequently shapes our behavior

Figure 3.1   Iceberg as Metaphor for Human Psyche

and thus we are often controlled by hidden imperatives that are buried deep in our psyches and of which we are unaware.

If many of our actions are based on our unconscious beliefs and attitudes, and marketers can discover these unconscious imperatives (the buttons that "turn us on," so to speak), they have a powerful tool that in theory can motivate us to behave in the ways they want us to behave. As Dichter points out, the knowledge we have of the way people can be motivated can be used for pro-social purposes, such as attacking racism and anti-Semitism, as well as for selling products and services.

Mary Douglas and Grid-Group Theory

Mary Douglas was a social anthropologist who developed grid-group theory to explain people's consumption practices and other kinds of behavior. Grid-group theory was also used by political scientist, Aaron Wildavsky—who often collaborated with Douglas—to explain people's voting, and it has been used by other social scientists for a variety of purposes.

Wildavsky drawing upon the work of Douglas explained that grid-group theory suggests that people continually find themselves asking two questions: the first question, "who am

I?" involves identity and the second question, "what should I do?" involves action or behavior. People answer the first question by becoming members of some group. Groups, grid-group theorists argue, have either very strong boundaries that limit an individual's entry and exit or have weak and porous boundaries, so people's ties to others are weak and choices bind only themselves. The answer to the second question, "what should I do?" involves whether there are a large number or a small number of prescriptions and rules that govern an individual's behavior.

Are people "free spirits" or "tightly constrained," as Wildavsky put it? The notion that groups are either strong or weak and that there are either few or many rules that govern their behavior leads to four groups or lifestyles: Fatalists, Elitists, Individualists, and Egalitarians (though Wildavsky sometimes changed the terms he used and Douglas used different terms for Egalitarians and Fatalists) (figure 3.2).

We can represent these groups in figure 3.3, which spells out the various relationships more directly.

What grid-group theory asserts is that there are only four groups or lifestyles (the term Douglas often uses) in all modern societies and that the elitists and individualists are the dominant groups in all societies. The egalitarians function as the critics of the social and political order, attempting to lift up the fatalists, who are subject to numerous rules and prescriptions and find themselves at the bottom of the socioeconomic ladder. In her

GROUP
Strength of Boundaries

		Weak	Strong
GRID *Number and* *Variety of* *Prescriptions*	**Many and Varied**	Fatalists	Elitists
	Few and Similar	Individualists	Egalitarians

Figure 3.2 Grid-Group Diagram
Source: Adapted from Wildavsky (1982).

Group Boundaries: Strong or Weak	Grid Aspects: Kinds and Number of Prescriptions	Ways of Life: Consumer Cultures
Strong	Numerous and varied	Elitist
Weak	Numerous and varied	Fatalist (Isolates)
Strong	Few or minimal	Egalitarian (Enclavists)
Weak	Few or minimal	Individualist

Figure 3.3 Grid-Group Theory and Lifestyles

seminal article "In Defence of Shopping," Douglas explains how these lifestyles relate to one another with a focus on the matter of consumption (1997:17–18):

> We have to make a radical shift away from thinking about consumption as a manifestation of individual choices. Culture itself is the result of myriads of individual choices, not primarily between commodities but between kinds of relationships. The basic choice a rational individual has to make is the choice about what kind of society to live in. According to that choice, the rest follows. Artefacts are selected to demonstrate that choice. Food is eaten, clothes are worn, cinema, books, music, holidays, all the rest are choices that conform with the initial choice of for a form of society.

A person's choice of what society to belong to (by which Douglas means which of the four lifestyles to identify with) shapes all future consumption choices, and the choice of a lifestyle involves hostility to other competing lifestyles. We make a mistake, Douglas argues, in focusing upon the wants people allegedly have. People never really know what they want but they always know what they *don't* want, which means they make their consumption choices based on their rejection of artifacts and other forms of consumption tied to other lifestyles.

This means that people's purchases are always made on the basis of their lifestyles and are always based on their identification with the group they belong to, which is, in turn, based on not buying the kind of things associated with other lifestyles. "Shopping," Douglas writes at the conclusion of her article, "is agonistic, a struggle to define not what one is, but what one is not. When we include not one cultural bias, but four, and when we allow that each is bring a critique against the others, and when we see that the shopper is adopting postures of cultural identity, then it all makes sense" (quoted in Pasi Falk and Colin Campbell, Eds., *The Shopping Experience*, 1997:30).

Her comment about shopping being agonistic is very similar to the statement Saussure made about concepts being differential. He wrote in his *Course in General Linguistics* (1915/1966:117), "concepts are differential and defined not by their positive content but negatively by their relations with the other terms of the system." Not only concepts, but also shopping and consumption in general, are differential. The other terms of the system for Saussure are equivalent to the other lifestyles for Douglas. Consumption may be done by individuals, Douglas argues, but it is not strictly a matter of individual choice.

New Strategist Publications

We have moved from universal theories about human motivation, as found in the work of Ernest Dichter, to theories about four all-important groups found in most modern societies. Marketers also focus upon age, race, ethnicity, gender, psychological makeup, and many other variables. What follows is a list of some of the books published by New Strategist Publications, which states "We're the demographers. Let us do the work for you." Many of these books are in their fifth, sixth, and eighth editions.

American Attitudes: Who Thinks What about the Issues That Shape Our Lives

A to Z Guide to American Consumers: Quick Links to Free Demographics

American Generations: Who They Are and How They Live
Who We Are: Asians
Who We Are: Blacks
Who We Are: Hispanics
American Time Use: Who Spends How Long at What
The American Marketplace: Demographics and Spending Patterns
Demographics of the U.S.: Trends and Projections
Household Spending: Who Spends How Much on What
The Millennials: Americans Born 1977 to 1994
Generation X: Americans Born 1965 to 1976
The Baby Boom: Americans Born 1946 to 1964
Older Americans: A Changing Market
Getting Wiser to Teens: More Insights into Marketing to Teenagers

You can see from this list that marketers have divided American society up many different ways. The publisher states, in its brochure, that it gets most of its data from the federal government and from the University of Chicago's National Opinion Research Center. What New Strategist does is organize the data it finds and make a number of calculations to information of interest to marketers. We can see, then, that marketers know a great deal about the behavior of American consumers, thanks to the data collected by the government and other research organizations.

New Strategist also sends monthly email reports for free. You can sign up to receive them at www.newstrategist.com.

Claritas Explains That "Birds of a Feather Flock Together"

Claritas is a marketing firm that has developed a typology, which divides American consumers into fourteen lifestyle groupings based on income and lifestyles, and sixty-six different consumer culture groupings based on ZIP Codes. They tend to give groups "catchy" names that are alleged to offer some insights into the nature of the groups. The fourteen lifestyles are in figure 3.4 that I have constructed from the information

Urban:
Urban Uptown. Midtown Mix. Urban Cores. Inner Suburbs.

Suburban:
Elite Suburbs. The Affluentials. Middle Blurbs. Rustic Living.

Second City:
Second City Society. City Centers. Micro City Blues.

Town & Country:
Landed Gentry. Country Comfort. Middle America.

Figure 3.4   Fourteen Lifestyles

on the Claritas website. They are arranged into four categories: Urban, Suburban, Second City, and Town & Country, listed according to income level, from the most affluent to the least affluent.

We can see that this list is geographic in nature and focuses upon where people live, and that those at the top of the chart are wealthier than those further down the list.

Claritas developed a more refined typology called PRIZM that lists sixty-six groupings. It describes PRIZM as follows (http://en-us.nielsen.com/tab/product_families/nielsen_claritas)

PRIZM operates on the principle that "birds of a feather flock together." It's a worldwide phenomenon that people with similar cultural backgrounds, needs, and perspectives naturally gravitate toward one another, choose to live in neighborhoods offering affordable advantages and compatible lifestyles. That's why, for instance, many young career singles and couples choose dynamic urban neighborhoods like Chicago's Gold Coast, while families with children prefer the suburbs which offer more affordable housing, convenient shopping, and strong local schools.

Claritas also obtains its information for the government and survey data. It argues that its data should be interpreted in a general way and not as an exact portrait of the lifestyles it deals with, which means it deals with purchasing preferences and not actual purchasing behavior. It focuses on ZIP Codes, where it provides as many as five different PRIZM clusters in a single ZIP Code, even though there may be as many as twenty different clusters found in that ZIP Code.

For Claritas, our identities are based on location: "You are where you live." Each ZIP Code covers from 2,500 to 15,000 households but the Claritas PRIZM groups deal with census block groups of between 250 and 500 households and its ZIP + 4 with from six to twelve households. Claritas claims to offer rather precise information about the consumption behavior of the different groups in its typology.

I should point out that many social scientists don't believe that "you are where you live," because of a number of factors. For example, in some wealthy suburban areas, a number of homeowners are "grandfathered in," which means they purchased their homes many years ago when the home were relatively inexpensive. I can speak about this matter based on personal experience. I purchased a home in Mill Valley, California (ZIP Code 94941-3519) in 1970, where homes like mine now cost around a million dollars, which is much more than I and most of my grandfathered-in neighbors could afford now. Mill Valley is located in Marin Country, one of the most affluent counties in the United States, located just five miles north of the Golden Gate Bridge. But Mill Valley is not as affluent as are other nearby Marin County towns, such as Ross and Belvedere, where houses may cost many millions of dollars.

A list of the Claritas sixty-six consumer cultures is shown in figure 3.5.

I checked my ZIP Code with Claritas and found that it deals with five groups living in it: "Upper Crusts," "Movers & Shakers," "Executive Suites," "Blue Blood Estates," and "Pools and Patios." Figure 3.6 shows how the Claritas 2007 version of PRIZM describes "Upper Crust" people.

01. Upper Crust
02. Blue Blood Estates
03. Movers & Shakers
04. Young Digerati
05. Country Squires
06. Winner's Circle
07. Money & Brains
08. Executive Suites
09. Big Fish, Small Pond
10. Second City Elite
11. God's Country
12. Brite Lites, Li'l City
13. Upward Bound
14. New Empty Nests
15. Pools & Patios
16. Bohemian Mix
17. Beltway Boomers
18. Kids & Cul-de-Sacs
19. Home Sweet Home
20. Fast-Track Families
21. Gray Power
22. Young Influentials
23. Greenbelt Sports
24. Up-and-Comers
25. Country Casuals
26. The Cosmopolitans
27. Middleburg Managers
28. Traditional Times
29. American Dreams
30. Suburban Sprawl
31. Urban Achievers
32. New Homesteaders
33. Big Sky Families
34. White Picket Fences
35. Boomtown Singles
36. Blue-Chip Blues
37. Mayberry-ville
38. Simple Pleasures
39. Domestic Duos
40. Close-in Couples
41. Sunset City Blues
42. Red, White, & Blues
43. Heartlanders
44. New Beginnings
45. Blue Highways
46. Old Glories
47. City Startups
48. Young & Rustic
49. American Classics
50. Kid Country, USA
51. Shotguns & Pickups
52. Suburban Pioneers
53. Mobility Blues
54. Multi-Culti Mosaic
55. Golden Ponds
56. Crossroads Villagers
57. Old Milltowns
58. Back Country
59. Urban Elders
60. Park Bench Set
61. City Roots
62. Hometown Retired
63. Family Thrifts
64. Bedrock America
65. Big City Blues
66. Low-Rise Living

Figure 3.5   The 66 Claritas Lifestyles

01, Upper Crust

Wealthy, Older w/o Kids

The nation's most exclusive address, Upper Crust is the wealthiest lifestyle in America—a haven for empty-nesting couples between the ages of 45 and 64. No segment has a higher concentration earning over $100,000 a year or possessing a postgraduate degree. And none has a more opulent standard of living.

Social group   Elite Suburbs
Lifestyle group   Affluent Empty Nests

2007 Statistics

U.S. households   1,733,015 (1.52%)
Median household income $111,546

Lifestyle Traits

Spend $3,000 + foreign travel
Shop at Bloomingdale's
Atlantic Monthly magazine
Golf Channel
Jaguar XK

Demographic Traits

Urbanicity   Suburban
Income   Wealthy
Income-producing assets   Elite
Age range   Ages 45–64
Presence of kids   Household w/o kids
Homeownership   Mostly owners
Employment levels   Professional
Education levels   Graduate plus
Ethnic diversity   White, Asian, Mix

Figure 3.6   Claritas on Upper Crust Group

It's interesting to see that this discussion of the lifestyle traits of the Upper Crust differs from one I found several years ago, where the lifestyle traits were: Contribute to PBS, Read *Architectural Digest,* Watch *Wall Street Week,* Drive a Lexus ES300 (www.mybestsegments.com).

The Claritas description of the people at the very bottom of the list is shown in figure 3.7.

66. Low-Rise Living
Low Income, Young w/ Kids

The most economically challenged urban segment, Low-Rise Living is known as a transient world for younger, ethnically diverse singles and single parents. Home values are low—about half the national average—and even less than a quarter of residents can afford to own real estate. Typically the commercial base of Mom-and-Pop stores is struggling and in need of a renaissance.

Social group	Urban Cores
Lifestage group	Sustaining Families

2007 Statistics

U.S. households	1,602,059 (1.41%)
Median household income	$23,540

Lifestyle Traits

Watch syndicated TV
Eat fast food burgers
Ebony Magazine
BET Network
Hyundai Accent

Demographic Traits

Urbanicity	Urban
Income	Low income
Income-producing assets	Low
Age range	Ages 25–44
Presence of kids	Mostly w/ kids
Homeownership	Renters
Employment levels	WD, Service, Mix
Education levels	Some high school
Ethnic diversity	White, Black, Hispanic

Figure 3.7 Claritas on Low-Rise Living

These portraits of the two groups are typical of the amount of detail about purchases, magazines read, and kinds of automobiles owned that are found in each of the groups. We can see that there are considerable differences between the members of the upper crust and low-rise living groups.

Claritas and other marketing groups know a great deal about what we have purchased and about what we are likely to purchase.

Each time a customer in a supermarket uses a credit card, information about that person's purchases is fed into a database. This means that Safeway (which is one of the supermarkets where I shop) knows a great deal about my preferences and everyone else's preferences (unless one pays by cash) for a variety of products. If you combine the information found in the databases in all the stores we visit and where we use credit cards, you get a very detailed picture of our consumption choices.

Complications for Marketers

There are a number of factors that complicate matters for marketers. One factor involves what is called "hybrid consumption," which requires companies to customize products. For example, if you order a Dell computer by telephone (or on the Internet), you can customize the computer and add extra memory, order different monitors, etc. which means that Dell has to spend more money catering to the tastes of its customers than if it simply manufactured a few different models. Another factor involves the globalization of markets and the competition from companies located in China and other countries. Many of the electronic products we purchase now, such as computers and cell phones, are manufactured in China, Taiwan, and other Asian countries with low labor costs.

One of the biggest problems involves the focus of marketing as it has evolved over the years. Some theorists, such as Peter Drucker, see marketing as a kind of strategic activity involving the economy, the minds of customers, and products, and don't like the narrow focus on selling products and brands that characterizes much of marketing now. As Drucker writes (quoted in Celia Lury, *Brands: The Logos of the Global Economy,* 2004:72):

> Marketing teaches that organized efforts are needed to bring an understanding of the outside, of society, economy and customer, to the inside of the organization and to make it the foundation for strategy and policy. Yet marketing has

rarely performed that grand task. Instead, it has become a tool to support selling. It does not start out with "who is the customer?" but "what do we want to sell?" It is aimed at getting people to buy the things you want to make.

Drucker may be harsh in his assessment, but his argument is worth considering. Instead of marketing being an effort to understand more about society and the economy and to use this information to target customers, Drucker argues that marketing has become essentially a means of selling products and of convincing people to want what companies want to sell. The main instrument used by marketers is the development of brands and brand awareness in people.

Greg Rowland suggests, in a personal communication, that creating these categories is self-serving for the marketing companies that generate them, because the more categories there are, the more advice clients need from the companies that originated the categories. He writes "It's much more efficient to get a few smart people in a room who know about the heritage of the brand, the popular culture that surrounds it, and generate a few ideas and later see, through qualitative techniques, if your target market (as broad as Young Mums 30–45) responds to any of the ideas positively."

Semiotics and Marketing Theory

When I started doing research for this book I was surprised to find that marketing scholars were very interested in semiotics and that a number of professors had written articles about using semiotic theory in marketing. In retrospect I shouldn't have been surprised because semioticians are constantly explaining that semiotics is the master science and can and must be used to understand just about every aspect of life. So, in retrospect, it was reasonable to assume that marketing academics (and professionals as well) might be interested in semiotics since it helps explain how we communicate ideas and attitudes to others, but I always thought that semiotics also had a somewhat dubious reputation (my colleagues often called it "idiotics" and made fun of my interest in signifiers and signifieds) and that many aspects of semiotic theory might not be of interest to marketers.

In a long review article about semiotics and marketing, "Pursuing the Meaning of Meaning," Mick, Burroughs, Hetzel, and Brammel (2004) write:

> This first section of our review reveals that semiotic design scholarship has flourished in countries and cultural regions where issues of style, form, fashion, and elegance have been historically central—most notably in France, Italy, Scandinavia, and Japan. The review also reveals that semiotics has unmistakably helped to address and partly resolve certain intellectual problems of meaning in product design. One specific contribution has been the development of new, sophisticated terms for conceptualizing the types and nature of signs that constitute a product and its potentiated meanings. To do this, some researchers have adopted and extended the Peircean distinctions of icon-index-symbol. Others have contributed to understanding the goals and processes of meaning generation in product design, based on Jakobson's renowned semiotic paradigm on the different roles of communication. The consumer influences of sign variations in product design (from Peirce or Saussure) have also been theorized in terms of recognition, comprehension, learning, memory, and appreciation (aesthetic reactions) at the product-type level and, occasionally, at the brand level.

The purpose of this article was to review the work that had been done on the relationship between marketing and semiotics, and it is one of the definitive analyses of the way semiotics can be used by marketers. As we can see, since semiotics deals with the way meaning is communicated, it plays a vital role in marketing. Many marketers actually function as applied semioticians even though they might never have heard of the science.

One of the most important aspects of marketing involves brands, which are the way products differentiate themselves from competitors. In the next chapter I discuss the role brands play in the way we form our identities.

PART II

Semiotic Applications

CHAPTER 4

Brands and Identity: We Are Our Brands

Branding has long been popular in consumer goods. Some brands have become so powerful that they are used as generic terms for the product itself. Aspirin, shredded wheat, and cellophane were all brand names at one time. The real growth of branding came after the Civil War, with the growth of national firms and national advertising media. Some of the early brands survive, notably Borden's, Quaker Oats, Vaseline, and Ivory soap...A *brand* is a name, term, sign, symbol, design, or a combination of these elements that is intended to identify the goods and services of a seller and differentiate them from those of competitors. A brand name is the part of the brand that can be vocalized. Examples are Disneyland, Hilton, Club Med, and Sizzler. A brand mark is the part of a brand that can be recognized but is not utterable, such as a symbol, design, or distinctive coloring or lettering...A trademark is a brand or part of a brand that is given legal protection; it protects the seller's exclusive rights to the use the brand name or brand mark.

Philip Kotler, John Bowen, James Makens,
Marketing for Hospitality and
Tourism (2nd edition)

Before examining the roles of brand in our forming an identity, let me say something about the nature of fashion, since brands are intimately connected to fashion and its various functions.

Fashion and Identity

In his book *Collective Search for Identity*, sociologist Orrin E. Klapp discusses the fashions in the 1960s, and though his focus is on fashions of fifty years ago, his description of the functions of fashion still applies. He writes (1962:75–76):

Several things seem new (in degree, if not in kind) and especially significant among the fashion expressions of the 1960s:

1. the sheer variety of "looks" (types) available to the common man;
2. the explicitness of identity search (for the "real you");
3. ego-screaming: the pleas "look at me!";
4. style rebellion (style used as a means of protest or defiance);
5. theatricalism and masquerading on the street;
6. pose as a way of getting to the social position one wants;
7. dandyism: (Living for style), turning away from the Horatio Alger (hard work, productivity) model of success;
8. dandyism of the common man as well as of the aristocrat;
9. pronounced escapism in many styles (such as those of beatniks, hippies, surfers, and in language such as "cool" and "freak out");
10. a new concept of the right to be whatever one pleases, regardless of what others think (the new romanticism);
11. the breakdown of status symbols, the tendency of fashions to mix and obscure classes rather than differentiate them;

12. the pursuit of status symbols reaching the dead end of a vicious circle breaking down meaning and making it hard to tell who is who.

This list covers the many functions of fashion and helps us understand the significance of fashion items and brands we use to send messages to others about who we are and what we are like.

He adds that increasing leisure has made it possible for all kinds of identity adventures and escapes through fashion to spread to large numbers of people. He writes (1962:74):

> The upshot is that status symbols are less often reminding people who they are and where they belong, and more often expressing a claim or wish to be somebody else. The range of material subject to fashion—that can be used as dramatic props, so to speak, for a new life—seems to be widening too: automobiles, gadgets, hobbies, foods, beverages, art, music, books, topics of conversation, slang, points of view, types of medical treatments—anything that can figure in one's life style as a status symbol.

The point is, then, that our understanding of the way people create identities for themselves through style is much broader than the clothes they wear. All the things that Klapp mentions can be seen, semiotically speaking, as signifiers of their lifestyles and claims to an identity.

Georg Simmel, the great German sociologist, explained that fashion has a double valence. On the one hand, it separates and differentiates us from others; on the other hand, it integrates us into society as well as into groups and subcultures with which we share similar tastes. He argues that as soon as the masses start adapting fashions used by the elites, they reject that fashion and search for something new, so the process of changes in styles never ends. One way that elites commonly differentiate themselves from others is through using global fashion brands, although the existence of imitations and knockoffs makes this practice increasingly more difficult.

Semiotics and Brands

From a semiotic perspective, brands are signifiers (often in the form of icons) companies use to establish their identities. Brands generate ideas and notions we have, generally provided by advertising but also by word of mouth, about the qualities of certain products and, by implication, the way they differ from competing products. Brands, then, are pure connotation, based on perceived and distinctive qualities a product has. Saussure said, "in language there are only differences." Semiotically speaking, we can say, "in brands, there are only differences"; the opposite of a brand is a generic product or one that has become a commodity.

In an article "Semiotics and Strategic Brand Management," Laura R. Oswald, a professor at the University of Illinois, discusses the role of semiotics in creating brands (www.media. illinois.edu/advertisng/semiotics_oswald.pdf):

> Over the past ten years or so, brand strategy researchers have come to recognize the importance of brand communication in building and sustaining brand equity, the value attached to a brand name or logo that supercedes product attributes and differentiates brands in the competitive arena... The contribution of brand meanings and perceptions to profitability—the Coca Cola brand is valued at over $70 billion—testifies to the power of symbolic representation to capture the hearts and minds of consumers by means of visual, audio, and verbal signs. The semiotic—or symbolic—dimension of brands is therefore instrumental for building awareness, positive associations, and long-term customer loyalty, and contributes to trademark ownership

and operational advantages such as channel and media clout. Consequently, managing brand equity means managing brand *semiotics*.

What Oswald points out is that it is semiotic theory that enables us to best understand how brands work and the role they play in consumer decision making.

We can see the difference between brands and their polar opposite, nonadvertised store brand products—that is, commodities—in figure 4.1.

The essence of branding lies in the claims a product have to being distinctive and having special attributes not found in competing products. The most common way that products get their identity is from advertising, which adds to the cost of the product. Some products are integrated into films and television programs, a practice known as product placement. The products pay to be shown in these texts, so product placements can be considered a form of advertising. In some cases, a celebrity or prominent person wears a product that becomes popular, such as when the Republican vice presidential candidate Sarah Palin wore a certain brand of Japanese eyeglasses. Many people who liked the look of the glasses then purchased that brand of eyeglasses. Nonbranded products don't advertise as a rule and are purchased on the basis of their functionality; they are, sociologically speaking, functional alternatives to branded products. What's important about brand name products is that they help confer identity upon those who use them.

Branded Product	Commodity
Distinctive	Functional
Expensive	Cheap (less expensive generally)
Advertised	Store brands: price sells
Confers identity	Saves money

Figure 4.1 Branded and Store Brand Products

Sociologist Celia Lury's book, *Brands*, offers a comprehensive view of brands and their impact upon consumer societies. Lury writes (2004:i):

> Brands are everywhere: in the air, on the high street, in the kitchen, on television and, maybe on your feet. But what kinds of things are they?

The brand, a medium of exchange between company and consumer, has become one of the key cultural forces of our time and one of the most important vehicles of globalization. In a new approach that uses media theory to study the economy, Lury offers a detailed and innovative analysis of brands. Her book argues that brands (this list is my construction):

1. mediate the supply and demand of products and services in a global economy;
2. frame the activities of the market by functioning as an interface;
3. communicate interactively, selectively promoting and inhibiting communication between producers and consumers;
4. operate as a public currency while being legally protected as private property in law;
5. introduce sensation, qualities and affect into the quantitative calculations of the market;
6. organize the logics of global flows of products, people, images and events.

Lury, who teaches at Goldsmiths, University of London, suggests that brands play a major role in contemporary societies on a global scale. It is her comment about brands generating sensations and affect, offering a semiotic portrait of the branded individual, that I will focus upon in this chapter.

Style Choices and Identity

In this investigation, I will deal with some of the more important products people can purchase as a means of forming their identities, and will cover such topics as hats, hair products (and styling), eyeglasses and sunglasses, ties, and shoes. All of these products are style choices can be looked upon as messages about ourselves that we send to others and to ourselves, to help establish an identity. We know that our identities are, in large measure, formed by feedback we get from others, and this feedback is shaped to a considerable degree by our style and brand choices. Many of our choices about these matters are shaped by our exposure to advertising and to various fads, crazes, and other kinds of collective behavior that play an important role in our purchasing decisions.

Hats

Consider the messages generated by top hats (which are hardly ever worn in the United States), berets, knit hats, fedoras and wide-brimmed hats, baseball caps, cowboy hats, and yarmulkahs. All of these are kinds of hats and each of them signifies different things. In figure 4.2, I list various kinds of hats and suggest, in broad and conventionally understood terms, what they signify.

Top hats, curiously, suggest upper-class status, but, ironically, they were also worn by chimney sweeps in Victorian Britain. Top hats are part of formal attire and are conventionally worn with tuxedos with tails, all of which are connected to formal and high status events. In the opening scenes of the cult television show *The Prisoner*, the man who gasses the hero is shown wearing a top hat, suggesting he is part of the British establishment. Berets are signifiers that have many meanings. Black berets were often worn by artists to suggest they are creative individuals, and colored berets are now worn by soldiers in many different armies. We conventionally see berets as signifying "Frenchness," but people in Spain, Belgium, and other countries wear them as well, so maybe "European-ness"

Signifier (Kind of Hat)	Signified (Conventional)
Top hats	Formality, upper-class status or ironically, chimney sweep in Victorian England
Berets	Arty, French culture
Knit hats	Functionality, also worn by skiers and criminals in jails
Wide-brimmed hats	Adventurer, nature lover, hiker
Baseball hats	Baseball lover but widely worn
Baseball with brim in back	Hip hop, coolness
Cowboy hat	The American West, cowboys
Yarmulke	Jewish religion

Figure 4.2   Hats as Signifiers

Bailey Western	Helen Kaminski
Kromer	Stormy
Bailey	Kangol
Tilley	Timberland
Betmar	New Era
Borsalino	Pantropic
Country Gentlemen	Plaza Suite
Eddy Brothers	Stetson

Figure 4.3   Brands of Hats

is more accurate. In the American context, berets might be seen as signifiers of being a foreigner or an artist.

When we come to wide-brimmed hats, we have to distinguish between hats with a few inches of brim (brands such as Borsalino, Panama hats) and very wide-brimmed hats, (worn by Indiana Jones in the movies and by adventurers, would-be adventurers, hikers, and others). Baseball caps are not branded by their manufacturers but many are branded by different baseball teams or are often used by companies to spread their name. At www.hats.com we find a list (figure 4.3) of the name brands they carry.

Borsalino hats sell for between $197.99 and $274.99 and Stetson hats range from $75 to $179.95, so we can see that brand name hats can be a rather expensive fashion accessory. On the

Sigmund Freud

other hand, you can purchase knit hats in drug stores for a dollar or two and baseball caps for a few dollars or so.

In "A Connection Between a Symbol and a Symptom" (in Philip Reiff, *Freud: Character and Culture*, New York: Collier Books) Sigmund Freud offers a psychoanalytic explanation of the significance of hats. He explains (1963:155–156):

> The HAT has been adequately established as a symbol of the genital organ, most frequently of the male, through analysis of dreams. It cannot be said, however, that this symbol is at all an intelligible one. In phantasies and in numerous symptoms the head also appears as a symbol of the male genitals, or, if one

prefers to put it so, as a representative of them. Many analysts will have noticed that certain patients suffering from obsessions express an abhorrence of and indignation against the penalty of beheading, feelings which are far more pronounced as regards this than any other form of capital punishment, and will in consequence have had to explain to them that they treat being beheaded as a substitute for being castrated.

If Freud is correct, the hat has, at the unconscious level, a much deeper and more profound significance for our psyches than we imagine and is connected with anxieties about castration.

Hair

Hair is an unusual part of our bodies because it is most easily manipulated in terms of its styling and its color. The hair industry, comprising both styling and color, is enormous. Everywhere in the world that I've traveled I've seen countless "beauty" salons. I don't think it is an understatement to say that many people are obsessed with their hair. In my files I discovered an old clipping, "Modern Rapunzels: Women and Their Hair," which states that a typical "woman combs, brushes or checks here hair five times a day, which takes her a total of 36 minutes.... The average woman goes to the hairdresser 13 times a year. Women over 50 go an average of 18 times a year; women under 50 visit the beauty shop about once a month." This clipping is quite old so the statistics are probably a bit dated, but the article, based on studies made by the Upjohn Hair Information Center, shows that woman spend a great deal of time and money on their hair.

In the United States, according to data on www.mindbranch. com that deals with shampoos and conditioners, we spend around $4.1 billion a year on personal hair products. This figure doesn't include money spent by salons and soaps that also can be used for shampooing hair. According to the report on mindbranch.com, the shampoo industry is a mature one, so

$600 million	Gels and mousses
$700 million	Hairsprays
150 million	Men's hair products
400 million	Permanents, hair-straightening products

Figure 4.4 Expenses for Hair Products in the United States

most of the focus among competing brands is on products that deal with specific hair problems. Figure 4.4 shows statistics on related hair products come from www.haircare.suite101.com on annual expenses for hair in the United States.

In the United Kingdom, it is estimated that people spend $50,000 over a lifetime on their hair. In a typical year, a person spends the equivalent of (in U.S. dollars):

$160 Shampoos
$120 Home styling
$520 Haircuts and styling

We can see, then, that the hair business is a huge one, which explains why women's magazines are full of advertisements for shampoos and hair-coloring products.

Folklore, Myths, and Hair

We can gain a sense of the importance hair plays in our consciousness by recognizing that in the Western world we have some important myths and folktales about hair, namely, stories about Rapunzel and Medusa. Rapunzel was imprisoned in a tower with no stairs by a witch who came to visit her by having Rapunzel let her hair down. A prince saw this and asked Rapunzel to let her long hair down for him, so he could climb up and visit her. This led, eventually, to their getting married and living happily ever after.

Medusa was a monster with snakes for her hair. Whoever looked at Medusa was turned to stone. She was killed by Perseus, who used his shield as a mirror and cut off her head without looking directly at her. I have suggested that women have what I call "the Medusa complex" and feel that their hair will, metaphorically speaking, "knock 'em dead" and thus contribute in important and positive ways to the way others—both men and women—see them. What these stories suggest is that our hair, and the way we style it and color it, play an important role in the way we develop our identities and the way others see us and think about us. Our hair has been of concern to us for thousands of years, and "bad hair days" are nothing new.

A Semiotic Approach to Hairstyles in the Eighties

In 1980, there was an article by the business editor, Donald White, in *The San Francisco Chronicle* titled "Office Life: Executives Can Lose by a Hair." The article dealt with hairstyles and the business world. White referenced a poll of 200 hairstylists in the San Francisco Bay area about what they considered to be the worst hairstyles of business executives. Figure 4.5 is a chart I made based on the findings of this poll. These analyses reflect the ideas the hairstylists have about hairstyles—ideas that probably reflect

Male Hairstyles **Signifiers**	**Meaning of Hairstyles** **Signifieds**
Crew cut	Old-fashioned, inflexible
Hair parted to hide baldness	Phoniness, self-consciousness
Shoulder-length hair	Antiestablishment values
Greased hair	Too slick, not trustworthy
Curly permanent grown out	Sloppy, disinterested

Female Hairstyles **Signifiers**	**Meaning of Hairstyles** **Signifieds**
Back-combed, bouffant	Archaic, can't embrace new ideas
Feathered in front, long in back	Teenybopper, lack of maturity
Severely streaked	Cheapness, low morals
Long hair, same length all around	Lack of personality and warmth
Punk rock	Anti-authority, belligerence

Figure 4.5   Male and Female Hairstyles as Signifiers and Signifieds

commonly held opinions and attitudes about the meaning of different hairstyles.

According to Linda Quigley, a fashion coordinator for a company with hairstyling stores who took the poll, many middle-level executives wear their hair in styles that suggest they are weak and ineffective and have other negative attributes. What this article suggests is that our hairstyles and hair colors are messages about our status and personalities that we send to others, even though we may not be fully aware of the role that our hairstyles and hair color play in our business and social lives.

Blondeness: The Importance of Hair Color

At one time, some seventy percent of the women in the United States who dyed their hair became blondes; now only around thirty-five percent do so. Around five percent of American women are natural blondes. If you add up these figures, you find that around forty percent of American women are blonde now. The reason they dye their hair blonde is that blondeness has positive symbolic and cultural meanings for Americans and others and is associated with glamour (think Marilyn Monroe and many other movie stars and celebrities), innocence, and fun. A study in England, financed by a hair-coloring company, found that women who dyed their hair blonde felt more confident and were more assertive.

Women often dye their hair blonde to cover gray hair or to escape from their ethnic identities. But there are other reasons as well. In his book, *The New People*, sociologist Charles Winick deals with some generally unrecognized aspects of becoming a blonde. He writes (1968:169):

> ...for a substantial number of women, the attractiveness of blondeness is less an opportunity to have more fun that the communication of a withdrawal of emotion, a lack of passion. One reason for Marilyn Monroe's enormous popularity was that she was less a tempestuous temptress than a nonthreatening

child…D. H. Lawrence pointed out that blonde women in American novels are often cool and unobtainable, while the dark women represent passion. Fictional blondes also tend to be vindictive and frigid.

So there are many different aspects to blondeness to consider, and dying one's hair blonde may be a message from one's unconscious about hiding one's true feelings about sexuality. Blondes are fun but they are also often thought of as frigid. If D. H. Lawrence is correct, a dark-haired woman who dyes her hair blonde has the passion of dark-haired women but visually the coolness of blonde women. Dying one's hair blonde may be an attempt to adopt a new and colder attitude toward sexuality.

An article by Lois Joy Johnson called "The New Hair Color Rules" quotes Brad Johns of the Elizabeth Arden Salon in New York City (*More*, July/August 2007:68):

> "If you're thinking red, go blonde. Red hair, unless it's natural, is tough on mature skin tones. It will expose and exaggerate blotchiness, brown spots or sallow undertones. But a honey blonde with golden tones works every time.

There are also brief articles on hair for women of color (to protect chemically straightened hair, use gentle color and leave it on for half the suggested time), gray hair (gray hair requires packaging, or your look can slip from great to granny) and brown hair (your twenty-something shade won't work when you're fifty). Because men and women can style their hair and change their hair color, hair remains a subject that ranges from mild concern to overpowering obsession. The fact that we call salons where people have their hair styled and colored "beauty parlors" suggests the unconscious significance of hair to men and women of all ages.

Designer Eyeglasses and Sunglasses

At one time, people who wore eyeglasses were ridiculed as being "four eyed" and were subject to negative attitudes in the general public. In Cambodia, the Khmer Rouge killed people who wore glasses, assuming that they were "intellectuals." Now, eyeglasses have become fashion accessories, and people spend a good deal of time and money finding the eyeglasses that they like and that convey the right messages about their taste and style. In an age in which everything we wear or carry with us is mined for its semiotic significance, eyeglasses now are important fashion items. Many advertisements for eyeglasses are close-ups of beautiful women and handsome men wearing glasses with the designer's logo or name on it. An ad for Dolce & Gabbana in the Fall 2008 issue of *WSJ* has an extreme close-up of a man wearing eyeglasses, and the name Dolce & Gabbana is clearly visible on the temples (the part of the glasses attached to the hinges and go behind the ears) of the eyeglasses. People who need to wear glasses but don't like the way they look with glasses now use contact lenses, though most people who wear contact lenses also have eyeglasses. Some people who don't need to wear glasses wear ones with clear lenses because glasses are a way of showing one's sense of style.

Over the years, certain styles of eyeglass frames become popular and other styles lose their popularity. Aviator-style glasses were popular a number of years ago, and then were deemed "square" by fashion arbiters, suitable for clerks, accountants, and other noncreative types. For a few years very large eyeglasses were popular, but in recent years small eyeglass frames have become fashionable. When Sarah Palin was nominated to be a vice presidential candidate, her $375 rimless glasses (designed by Kazuo Kawasaki, style series 704, color 34) became very popular for a short time. Then people became disillusioned with her, and she became a butt of jokes and impersonations by Tina Fey, who used the Kawasaki glasses to great effect.

Sunglasses are another way that people can show their sense of style. These glasses have the benefit (for manufacturers) of being able to be worn by people who don't need to wear prescription glasses. An advertisement for Louis Vuitton sunglasses, in which a woman puts on and takes off her sunglasses, shows five symbols related to Vuitton. Because frames come in so many styles and colors, there are an enormous number of possible choices. The development of transition lenses bridges the gap between conventional glasses and sunglasses, for they are both conventional eyeglass lenses and sunglass lenses. These glasses become dark when exposed to direct sunlight. How dark they become is a matter of choice by the person who purchases the lenses.

Dark eyeglasses enable people to "hide" behind their lenses and observe what is going on around them without anyone being able to look into their eyes. These glasses generate a kind of detachment that can vary from a mild degree of hiding to alienation. Tourism scholars have described what they call the "tourist gaze" as a means for tourists to psychologically dominate people in foreign lands who are the recipients of this gaze. The tourist gaze can be hidden, to a degree, by wearing dark sunglasses.

Teeth

A San Francisco cosmetic dentist made the front page of *The Wall Street Journal* a number of years ago. He argued that professional men and women are often judged by those who hire or employ them by their teeth. In an article by Marilyn Chase, titled "Your Suit Is Pressed, Hair Neat, But What Do Your Molars Say?" Dr. Jeffrey Morley offered his interpretations of what teeth reveal about people:

> What it comes down to is this: Buck teeth imply people are dumb. Large canines imply aggressiveness. Weak chins imply passivity, while strong chins imply a macho, studly personality. I don't know who made these up, but the fact is, they're cultural standards.

This struck the reporter from *The Wall Street Journal* as quite remarkable, but this article appeared on June 16, 1982 when people were less aware of the importance of semiotics and of the numerous ways in which people "read" other people for clues to their character and socioeconomic status. The fact is, teeth are read as signs by people, and people with yellow teeth, uneven teeth, missing teeth, and large canines are evaluated by others, often unconsciously. We may not be aware of judging people by their teeth, but if Morley is correct, we cannot avoid doing so.

This matter of "reading" teeth may explain why a huge industry for whitening teeth has developed. It is possible to purchase a number of products that will allow people to whiten their teeth—white teeth being a sign that we care about our appearance. Every time we smile, we show our teeth, and people we are with or who see us react to our teeth. Dr. Morley had a friend who was an orthodontist. When I met with Dr. Morley, his associate offered to break my jaw and push my chin forward, since he thought my chin wasn't "studly" enough. Our concern about our teeth has also generated many products devoted to keeping our teeth clean and avoiding cavities and plaque. We can purchase any number of different brands of toothpaste, electronic toothbrushes, floss, and all kinds of other products designed to protect our teeth and make them more attractive.

Some sociologists use a theatrical metaphor to describe the way we behave. From this perspective, we are all actors, and our relations with others take on the characteristics of a theatrical performance. Sociologist Erving Goffman describes this phenomenon in his book, *The Presentation of Self in Everyday Life* and suggests we all have "personal fronts" that we use in our performances. He writes, "As part of personal front we may include: insignia of office or rank, clothing, sex, age, and racial characteristics; size and looks; posture, speech patterns; facial expressions; bodily gestures; and the like" (1959:23–24).

Our teeth play a role in what Goffman calls our "looks" and in our facial expressions. Whenever we open our mouths, others (people to whom we are speaking or who are looking at us) can see our teeth and they are affected by the way our teeth look. Morley's argument was that people who apply for high-paying positions need to recognize that it is a worthwhile investment to ensure that their teeth are perfect so that they make a good impression on those who are thinking of hiring them. Many middle- and upper-class children in wealthy countries sport braces, indicating that they are going to an orthodontist who is straightening their teeth and fixing their bite. Drugstores are full of products and devices we use to clean our teeth, from simple toothbrushes to expensive electronic toothbrushes.

Wristwatches

Wristwatches have become important fashion accessories for many people. Although the main purpose of wristwatches is to tell the time, in actuality they have a more important function with many men and women—as indicators of stylishness, discrimination, and socioeconomic class. If you look through any magazine directed toward upscale—that is, wealthy—consumers, you see numerous advertisements for extremely expensive watches. Some of these watches sell for many hundreds of thousands of dollars and tend to function like jewelry, as indicators of status and wealth for the superrich who can afford them.

In the December 2008 issue of *Forbes Life*, we find a number of advertisements for expensive mechanical watches:

> Cartier Roadster
> Hermes ("A Hermes watch has time on its side")
> Glashutte: The Panoinverse XL
> Tourbillon
> Breitling Bentley 6.75 Chronograph (Power. Luxury. Exclusivity.)
> Schaffhausen
> Jacob & Co.
> Bell & Ross
> Salvatore Ferragamo F-80
> Zenith

In addition to these advertisements for watches, there was an article on enamel watches, "The Enamel Cult," that featured such mechanical watches as:

Vacheron Constantin ($79,000)
Breguet Classique Chronograph (white, $42,000; gold, $41,500)
Patek Philippe World Time ($53,700)

Piaget Polo Tourbillon Relatif ($481,000)
Van Cleef & Arpels Tourbillon Paon ($285,000)
Ulysse Nardin Tellurium (gold, $99,000; platinum, $150,000)
Jaquet Droz Petite Heure Minute Paillonee ($36,400)

We can see, then, that these watches are not sold based on their ability to tell time but rather on their ability to serve as fashion and status symbols and style statements for the extremely wealthy or the superrich, who are the only people who can afford watches that cost $285,000. In some cases, these watches are now purchased by collectors. Collecting these kinds of watches is a very expensive undertaking.

The development of digital watches led to the demise, more or less, of mechanical watches; most people who wear watches wear digital ones now. These watches can be purchased for as little as $15.00, and some cheap watches from China are much less than that. My most recent watch is a Casio that I purchased for $11.00. I will now compare and contrast digital watches with mechanical watches to provide some insights into the social and cultural significance of each kind of watch, dealing with watches at both ends of the cost spectrum; that is, expensive mechanical watches and cheap digital watches (figure 4.6).

Mechanical watches, even relatively modestly priced ones, are much more complicated than digital watches, which are powered by a small battery and use a quartz mechanism to indicate the time, the date, and do other things. Some watches combine

Mechanical Watches	Digital Watches
Machines	Devices
Mechanical	Electronic
Old-fashioned	Modern
Expensive	Cheap
Status basic	Function basic

Figure 4.6 Mechanical and Digital Watches Compared

mechanical and quartz elements. If telling time were the only function of watches, everyone would wear digital watches, since they are cheap and keep the time very well. They first appeared in the early 1960s. With some early digital watches, you had to press a button to get the time, some psychologists who studied people using these watches suggested that being able to summon time gave people a sense of power. Digital watches signify important changes that have taken place in the world, as digital devices have replaced mechanical and electromechanical devices in many products.

In his book *The Digital Dialectic*, Peter Lunenfeld defines digital as follows (1999:xv–xvi):

> Digital systems do not use continuously variable representative relationships. Instead, the translate all input into binary structures of 0s and 1s, which can then be stored, transferred, or manipulated at the level of numbers or "digits" (so called because etymologically, the word descends from the digits on our hands with which we count out those numbers). Thus a phone call on a digital system will be encoded as a series of these 0s and 1s and sent over the wires as binary information to be reinterpreted as speech on the other end.

With an analog watch, you see relationships—how many minutes remain before an hour or after an hour. With a digital watch, you see an indication of the time at a given moment. In the digital age, time becomes a succession of discrete moments indicated on your watch. To the extent that analog suggests relationships and digital suggests separation (of time into discrete moments), we can say that digital suggests a sense of alienation from others and from society. And as digital devices proliferate, and people walk around wired and listening to their MP3 players or cell phones, you do sense that there is a diffuse kind of alienation engendered by these devices. That might explain why people make so many calls on their cell phones—to counter the separation and alienation they feel, which is engendered by digital devices.

What has happened in recent years is that wristwatches have become an important accessory for people who wish to demonstrate their taste and discrimination as well as their purchasing power or wealth. In some cases, people use these watches to hide their wealth and dressing "poor" is the way they do this. Ironically, because of the popularity of cell phones, many people no longer wear wristwatches, since they can find out what time it is from their cell phones.

The cell phone has eclipsed the wristwatch as an indicator of being modern and hip and has replaced wristwatches for many people, just as the wristwatch replaced the pocket watch many years ago. The best known wristwatch is the Rolex, which is considered one of the top one hundred global brands in the world by an organization that ranks brands. Rolex watches can be had for around $10,000, which makes them, relatively speaking, a bargain in the realm of expensive watches, but their popularity means that they don't have the same cachet of the more expensive watches. Rolex watches are indicators, it would seem, of upper-middle-class status or lower-upper-class status.

Facial Hair in Men

In the past year several friends of mine have shaved off their mustaches. When I asked them why, I got vague answers such as "I got tired of my mustache" or "I decided I looked better without it." Mustaches are more common than beards. Not so long ago, beards suggested probity and seriousness, but in recent years everyone from Hell's Angels to adolescents and young men playing with their identities have sported beards. In the gym where I work out, one of the trainers spent months growing a beard, shaving it off, then growing it again; he couldn't decide whether he looked better in his beard. In some cultures, most of the men wear mustaches. In a recent trip to India, our driver had a luxuriant mustache that was a source of great pride to him. Once, when we had stopped for a red light, two men on a motorcycle next to our car told him how great his mustache was. He was delighted. "Nowadays," our driver said, "many men feel mustaches are old fashioned and so men in India who want to be modern no longer wear them."

Facial hair, we must recognize, is a signifier of masculinity. Mustaches and beards are one way that men can clearly indicate their gender. Having facial hair is particularly important for men with long hair; otherwise, it is possible to mistake their gender when seeing them from a distance or from the back. We see male models in fragrance ads, often with a day or two of hair growth that signify their masculinity.

Men who have mustaches and beards can purchase trimmers to keep their mustaches and beards under control. In some societies, many men just let their beards and mustaches grow without trimming them, but in modern countries men often trim their mustaches and beards, opening up a market for companies to manufacture different kinds of trimmers. On the Internet I found the following products:

> Remington MB-300 Titanium Beard and Mustache Trimmer
> Wahl 9918-617 Groomsman Beard and Mustache Trimmer
> Stern Moustache Wax
> Stern Moustache Comb
> Stern Moustache Snood

And I found many other brands of trimmers and other products for mustaches and beards. If a man doesn't want a mustache and beard, he must shave. If he does want a mustache, a beard, or both, unless he likes the ragged beard look, he must purchase something to trim his hair with, whether it is a simple scissors or an electronic trimmer.

Fragrances

Perfumes and fragrances are products that emit odors deemed pleasant and thought to be sexually arousing. Women have used perfumes for thousands of years, but it is only in the last fifty or sixty years that men have been induced, thanks in great measure to advertising, to purchase fragrances. Now the term "fragrance" is often used for both perfumes for women and products for men. A creator of perfumes, Serge Lutens, defines perfumes as follows (www.mimifroufrout.com): "Perfume, in and of itself, is not just an aroma. It is potentially a carrier for the imagination. Perfume is thick; it is poison and pure desire. It is Eros in prison." Lutens calls our attention to perfume's erotic mission and its power to affect us in profound ways. It is, he explains, more than just being an aroma. It is magical, like poison, except that its function is sexual excitement and passion, not death.

A blog about perfumes, "Now Smell This," lists the brands and names of hundreds of perfumes. I have selected some of the more interesting or provocative perfume names, semiotically speaking, which I will treat as signifiers and consider their signifieds (figure 4.7).

What these names do for the women and men who wear them is suggest something about the identity of the wearer. The Beckham perfume is a "celebrity" perfume, while the others are from well-known fashion houses. A number of movie stars and celebrities, such as Elizabeth Taylor and Sarah Jessica Parker, have created perfumes or have had their names attached to perfumes. Some perfumes are named after the brand, such as Dolce & Gabbana's "Dolce & Gabbana" and Paul Sebastian's "Paul Sebastian."

Greg Rowland, a commercial semiotician who was involved with the creation of the Euphoria concept, explains that they

Brand of Perfume	Signifier/Name	Signifieds
Calvin Klein	Euphoria	Blissful well-being
Calvin Klein	Obsession	Compulsiveness
Chanel	L'Egoiste	Self-centeredness
David Beckham	Instinct	Unthinking behavior
Ungaro	Diva	Star who demands much attention
Giorgio Armani	Attitude	Sense of self's priorities
Lanvin behavior	Scandal	Morally offensive
Ralph Lauren	Notorious	Infamous and well-known

Figure 4.7 Names of Fragrances and Semiotic Implications

wanted to "capture some of the dark Ingmar Bergman type modernism that had differentiated the brand in the late 80s." This was lost in the 1990s, he adds, when the company started asking consumers what they wanted in a fragrance and got stock replies like "happiness" and "authenticity."

People who wear a brand name fragrance are identifying with the brand more than with the name of the product. Along with the brand extensions of products, we can suggest that many people are careful in their choices of perfumes and other fashion products and lifestyle signifiers, which explains what we mean by style—fashion and other choices that fit together logically into a coherent whole. Many perfumes are given French or Italian names because in the popular imagination, Italian products suggest luxury and refinement and French names suggest sophistication, sex, and elite culture.

Brand Narcissism and L'Oréal Fragrances

Charles Brenner's book, *An Elementary Textbook of Psychoanalysis*, discusses narcissism in a chapter on the psychic apparatus. He writes (1974:98):

In psychoanalytic literature the term "object" is used to designate persons or things of the external environment which are psychologically significant to one's psychic life, whether such things are animate or lifeless.

He then discusses the self-directed libido, which Freud designated as narcissism, based upon the Greek legend of Narcissus, who fell in love with himself. Narcissism is generally understood to be a disproportionate concern with oneself and one's image and, relative to consumer cultures, a desire for the good things of life and in some cases, an obsessive concern with objects, sometimes leading to fixations on certain kinds of products.

According to psychologists, we all need an element of narcissism in order to develop adequate self-esteem and to accomplish things in our lives. Many great creative artists, dancers, and musicians are narcissists, who have channeled their narcissism in constructive ways. The problem is that with some individuals narcissism dominates their lives, and certain characteristics associated with narcissism start becoming evident: a sense of superiority to others, self-centeredness, excessive self-interest, a constant need for adulation, anger and moody behavior when criticized, and a tendency to become depressed when failing in something. Freud's concept of "reaction formation" explains how it can be that some people mask their narcissism by devoting a great deal of energy to humanitarian causes and other kinds of selfless behavior. Finally, there is a kind of collective or group narcissism in which people derive esteem from identifying with winning sports teams or with American culture and a sense of "being number one."

The semiotician Greg Rowland suggests that there is what he describes as "brand narcissism" at work in consumer cultures. As he explains in his essay published in *Brand Strategy* magazine (February 2007):

It's important for brands to be aware of the complexities and contradictions around the Consumer Narcissus. Consumer culture encourages consumers to think of themselves as special, unique and wonderful people. But this process, sometimes fuelled by forms of over literal market research, can lead to a consumer tyranny wherein the hapless brand abandons core equities in knee-jerk responses to the whims of their consumer masters. We can never fully please the consumer. And this, ironically, is the key to the survival of the consumer economy. Consumer culture has constructed people that can never be fully satisfied by anything. But this infinite extension of desire is one of the pre-conditions for consumer culture to work effectively. We need to people to be relatively happy with their purchases, but not so happy that they don't continually explore new avenues of self-fulfilment through consumption. Consumer culture always leaves them wanting that little bit more, that indefinable something that will lead to genuine happiness.

Rowland argues that marketers have become dominated by research that blinds them to the emotional needs people have and the way they relate to products.

These marketers, he believes, rely too much on consumer opinion and neglect the symbolic and semiotic significance of many of the products they sell. He offers an example of a successful campaign, discussing the way L'Oréal sells its beauty products:

The celebrity is a useful organizing principle for people's concerns about glamour, identity, femininity and many other subjects. The right celebrity therefore serves up a perfect synecdoche for a brand's values for a brand's values—and the celebrities themselves realize this, and will demand fees according to their symbolic market values. And even news of the financial transactions and contracts between companies and celebrities becomes part of the branding exercise.

The typical celebrity spokeswoman communication varies between a suggestion of friendly advice and implied threat. At stake is the very conception of yourself as Narcissus: "because you're worth it." L'Oréal builds up out idea of self-esteem, but threatens to take it away by non-participation in the brand. The consumer needs to echo the Narcissism of the brand itself in their own purchase of the product, otherwise they are left as an empty husk who, it is implied, "is not worth it." This continuing psychodrama between a Brand Narcissus simultaneously empowering and threatening the Consumer Narcissus has clearly worked very well for L'Oréal over many years.

This advertising uses consumer narcissism effectively and puts beauty product users in a psychological bind that works out very well for L'Oréal, for users must purchase the L'Oréal product to demonstrate that they are "worth" it; otherwise they face a self-definition of not being "worth" it, or very much else.

Neckties

The design and color of neckties worn by presidents and other politicians is a subject of considerable interest to news commentators and others, who see ties as important indicators of the state of mind of the necktie wearer. Many politicians now wear red ties in various shades, which are seen as "power" neckties, in the same way that many women politicians now wear red "power" dresses and suits. In Britain, neckties can be used to indicate which public school (i.e., which private school) or university one attended, so ties there have an obvious function in indicating one's past educational affiliations and socioeconomic status. While some American universities have neckties with the school colors and symbols, this aspect of ties is not as important as it is in Britain. We also can indicate what universities we attended by our rings, but they are difficult for others to interpret.

There are different kinds of neckties to be considered as well. Bow ties, except those worn with tuxedos, are commonly associated with intellectuals and people who are independent and perhaps even a bit idiosyncratic in their tastes. String neckties are worn by those who wish to connect themselves to western American lifestyles. There are also fashion changes in neckties: In the fifties and sixties they were thin, but now they are much wider. Striped neckties convey a different message than do solid color or paisley ones. There is also the kind of knot one uses for tying a necktie.

Historically, wearing a necktie has been connected with self-restraint. In her book *Dress Codes: Meaning and Messages in American Culture*, Ruth P. Rubinstein writes (1995:41): "An essential element of male dress that is symbolic of holding one's feelings is the neckcloth or tie ... In the United States, it was not until the growth of bureaucracies in the 1940s that the tie emerged as required attire for 'white-collar' workers." Blue-collar workers do not usually wear ties. Rubinstein discusses the ideas of a journalist, Scott R. Schmedel, who explains that wearing a sport jacket, shirt, and tie demonstrates one has incorporated the "societal expectation of self-restraint" (1995:42).

Later in the book Rubinstein discusses the ideas of a fashion reporter on kinds of necktie wearers. Rubinstein writes (1995:68):

In pairing men with types of neckties, fashion reporter Ruth La Ferla identified four general categories of tie wearers: the collegian, the corporate worker, the cosmopolite, and the iconoclast. The collegian's tie is diagonally striped ribbed silk or embroidered with shields or heraldic insignia (club ties). It communicates that the student wearing it is ready to meet the scrutiny of a vigilant parent or headmaster.... The corporate worker's tie suggests "power, authority and unflappable decorum." Its message is conveyed by a suitably weighty pattern on a background of blue or claret-colored silk. The cosmopolite, more dashing than the corporate worker, wears solid-color satins or crisp knit ties. The rich luster of the fabric betrays a love of finery, La Ferla observed. Finally, the convention flouting iconoclast prizes wit and inventiveness about stiff propriety. He uses the tie to set the tone for the rest of his ensemble.

Rubinstein mentions a 1989 poll of American men, which indicated that they thought that a man's occupation and title was reflected in his choice of ties. They also believed that most CEOs wore silk ties and that their favorite color was blue. She also mentions a 1993 *Forbes Magazine* article that suggested that necktie styles can forecast economic trends. The article suggested that previous styles of ties were being supplanted by ones with natural or earth colors and by ones that had jewel tones and regular patterns, which were unconscious expressions of uneasy feelings about bad economic times. Understanding fashion images, she points out, involves connecting the styles of neckties and of fashion in general to the social, cultural, and economic context in which the styles are found. This means our ties not only reflect our personal taste and our sense of which conventions to follow in our dress, but also mirror in subtle ways our sense of optimism or pessimism about what is going on in society.

Men's neckties sell for various prices—from $4.00 at Briteties. com to $165 for Gucci neckties and $145.99 for Ferragamo neckties at Neckties.com. Some of the ties at the latter Internet site, for brands such as Principessa, sell for $24.99, and there are many other brands for similar prices. Neckties.com lists many categories of ties, such as "Artist," "Brand Name," "Conversational," "Floral," "Knit," "Narrow," "Plaid," "Polka Dot," "Solid," "Striped," and "Zipper" (which are zipped on instead of clipped on ties). There are 1,780,000 Internet sites that you find on Google if you type in "neckties," and you can find everything from silk ties for $4.00 to instructions on how to tie neckties. An article by *Newsweek* reporter Tony Dokoupil, "Political Ties: How Presidential Candidates Knot Their Neckties and What Is

Says About Them" (Oct. 14, 2008), suggests that it is the types of necktie knots used by the 2008 presidential candidates that was revealing. McCain favored a Windsor or half-Windsor, which was popular with Washington political elites; Obama, on the other hand, favored a four-in-hand knot, which indicated that there was a rebellious and aspirational quality to his character. So it isn't only the color and fabric and design and shape of the necktie, but the knot that is used that conveys messages to us as we "people watch" and attempt to read the signs they provide us through everything from their hairstyles and eyeglass designs to the way they knot their ties.

Shoes

From a functional perspective, we wear shoes to protect our feet from dirt, pebbles, and rain, and to keep them warm in cold weather and dry in wet weather. But shoes play an important role in the way we see ourselves and present ourselves to others—especially shoes worn by women, since these shoes have a powerful sexual dimension to them.

In his book, *The Sex Life of the Foot and Shoe*, William A. Rossi offers some insights into the sexual dimensions of the foot and shoes. He begins his book with a chapter titled "The Erotic Foot and the Sexual Shoe" (1976:1):

> The foot is an erotic organ and the shoe is its sexual covering... The human foot possesses a natural sexuality whose powers have borne some remarkable influences on all peoples of all cultures throughout all history. Podoerotica bears its influences on our everyday lives today.

So shoes are not simply coverings for our feet but are connected to our erotic sensibilities. Podoerotica is the term Rossi uses to describe the erotic aspects of feet and shoes. He offers a number of sexual aspects of the foot that lead him to his conclusions. I list some of them below in an abbreviated form.

It is one of our most sensitive tactile organs.

It has had an impact on the development our erogenous features such as the buttocks, bosom, legs, and thighs.

It led to the development of the human figure and is responsible for our upright posture and to frontal human copulation, which is unique in the animal kingdom.

Foot fetishism is the most common kind of sex-related fetishism.

The foot is responsible for the human gait and the most erotic aspects of women's anatomy and gait.

The physical contours of the foot have erotogenic powers.

As a result of the sexuality of the foot, we have such phenomena as foot binding among the Chinese for a thousand years, the creation of hundreds of thousands of shoe fetishists, and the development of a shoe industry that exists to enhance the sexual dimensions of the foot. Although we may not realize it, Rossi suggests (1976:13), "Shoes are designed and worn, consciously or subconsciously, to convey psychosexual messages...While the foot has always been a phallic symbol, the shoe has always been a yoni, or vulva, symbol. This male (foot) and female (shoe) relationship is both ancient and universal."

The shoe's role in folklore suggests its sexual dimensions. The folktale about Cinderella is resolved when the Prince she met at a ball uses her shoe to find her. There is also a sexual dimension to the custom of tying old shoes—that fit comfortably—to the back fenders of cars of men and women who are leaving on their honeymoons. The unconscious sexual significance of shoes may explain why choosing shoes is so difficult for many young women, since the shoes are signifiers of the unconscious sexual attitudes of the purchaser.

High heels, for example, tilt a woman's body forward slightly and change the way she walks and the way that her breasts are displayed. The physical cost to wearing high heels, some of which are now four and five inches high, is, according to Rossi, sadomasochistic. He uses the same term for pointed male shoes.

Women are willing to be uncomfortable if they think they are being sexually alluring and glamorous. Low heels, on the other hand, may be more comfortable but reflect a different perspective about sexuality; they are seen as sexless or nonsexual.

The aesthetic qualities of women's shoes lead some women to shoe fetishism, a sexual attachment to shoes as beautiful objects, and may explain Imelda Marcos's legendary collection of 3,000 pairs of shoes. Fetishism involves either a belief in the magical qualities of an object or the displacement of sexual desire from an individual to an object. Leland E. Hinsie and Robert Jean Campbell describe fetishes in their *Psychiatric Dictionary* (4th edition) as follows (1970:300):

> In psychiatry, the love object of the person who suffers from the perversion called fetishism—usually a part of the body or some object belonging to or associated with the love object. The fetish replaces and substitutes for the love object, and although sexual activity with the love object may occur, gratification is possible only if the fetish is present or at least fantasized during such activity. Typical also is the ability of the fetishist to obtain gratification from the fetish alone, in the absence of the love object. The most common fetishes—shoes, long hair, earrings, undergarments, feet— are penis symbols or serve to avoid complete nudity of the female....

The authors have a citation about foot fetishism under the term "retifism" that describes people such as French educator, Rétif de la Bretonne, who had a fetish about shoes and feet and "loved" female shoes, which he used for masturbating. Men with this perversion use objects they fetishize to substitute for an interest in female genitals.

The foot is a much more important part of the human body than we imagine, both from a physical standpoint—it contains a large number of bones—and also from a psychoanalytic standpoint. Some women can achieve orgasm by having their feet massaged. That might explain why choosing shoes becomes such a problem for men and women, though perhaps more so for women than men, since the foot plays such an important role in our unconscious erotic life and in our conscious sense of our sexual attractiveness.

Handbags and Messenger Bags

Handbags are one of the more popular accessories for women, and in recent years, they have become an important part of women's fashion in many countries. In Japan, young schoolgirls slip off their uniforms and sleep with middle-aged businessmen because the girls want to be able to afford expensive handbags. This practice is known in Japan as "compensated dating," and is now spreading to other countries. There seems to be a kind of addiction for handbags in women who place a good deal of importance on being "fashionable." There are, it turns out, a large number of books on handbags.

In one book, *Handbags: What Every Woman Should Know*, author Stephanie Paulson suggests that women should buy their handbag first and then build their outfits around them. This would suggest that handbags are the most essential consideration for women when they decide what to wear. According to Paulson, women need a number of different kinds of handbags. They need the following kinds of bags: an evening bag, for when they go to events where they want to look fashionable; a work bag, which should be functional and enable them to carry their cell phones and other gizmos to their jobs; a weekend "fun" bag, for casual events; and a gym bag. She defines fashion as "a fun way to express yourself."

In another book, *Handbags: The Power of the Purse*, Anna Johnson quotes Tom Ford on what women should look for in handbags. He was the Creative Director for Gucci at the time. As Ford explains, "If a bag is attractive, it makes you feel good by default. It's about proportion, shape, line, finish, fabric, balance. If all of that is pleasing it will sell. More than that it's like you gotta have it or you'll die." Why do women have this need to have handbags? Why do some of them feel, as Tom Ford puts it, they've "gotta have it" or they'll die? Women have used handbags for hundreds of years, as fashion accessories. What might be behind this craze in recent years?

To answer this question, let me say something about human sexuality, drawing upon material from Erik H. Erikson's book, *Childhood and Society* (2nd edition) and his work with "the manifestations of the power of organ modes in spatial modalities" (1963:99). He asked a large number of children to play with building blocks and discovered that boys tend to use blocks to build towers and girls tend to use blocks to build enclosures of one kind of another. His experience led to his assumption "that the modalities *common* to either sex may express something of the sense of being male or female" (1963:101). Boys, he discovered, built towers and girls built houses and other enclosures. He concluded that "high" and "low" are masculine variables and "open" and "closed" are female modalities. Boys build towers that reflected the "penetrating" modality of their sexual organs, and the constructions of the girls reflected what we could call the "incorporative" or "enclosing" modality of their sexual organs. Sexually speaking, we are led to conclude, males penetrate and females incorporate.

Erikson's findings correlate with ideas presented by Freud in his book, *A General Introduction to Psychoanalysis*. In his tenth lecture, on "Symbolism in Dreams," Freud writes (1924/1962:163–164):

The female genitalia are symbolically represented by all such objects as share with them the property of enclosing a space or are capable as acting as receptacles: such as *pits, hollows and caves*, and also *jars and bottles*, and *boxes* of all sorts and sizes, *chests, coffers, pockets,* and so forth. *Ships* too come into this category. Many symbols refer rather to the uterus than to all the other genital organs: thus *cupboards, stoves* and above all, *rooms.* Room symbolism here links up with that of houses, whilst *doors and gates* represent the genital opening...yet another noteworthy symbol of the female genital organ is a *jewel case....*

Freud is talking about symbolism in dreams whose meaning we generally do not recognize, but we can see that the incorporative modality is pervasive in sexual symbols about women. His mention of jewel cases brings his analysis very close to the subject of purses.

This discussion leads to a hypothesis about the psychoanalytic significance of women's handbags—they are, it can be suggested, unrecognized externalizations of the female incorporative sexuality. We can say, then, the handbag is a public representation of a woman's sense of her sexuality and of her sexual organs. That would explain why handbags have become such an important fashion accessory and why so many women spend so much psychic energy and income in choosing their handbags. Men have many pockets to put their things in, but women generally have to carry their cell phones, makeup, combs, brushes, and other things they use daily in some kind of a container, and for many women, a handbag is the container of choice. Men also carry briefcases and attaché cases, and in recent years, messenger bags, in which they can store things and while some women carry briefcases and attaché cases, they are generally used by professional women and are not widely used by women the way handbags are.

In the April 2, 2009 edition of *The New York Times,* there were a number of advertisements for more-expensive handbags, including Bergdorf Goodman's ad for Nancy Gonzalez bags ($2,850 to $5,235) and Chanel's Lambskin Classic bag ($2,695). There were also ads for bags by Gucci and Kate Spade, but they didn't have prices listed. Handbags have become, like mechanical watches, very expensive accessories, although knockoffs of many designer handbags are available for relatively little money.

Brand Extensions and Lifestyle Signifiers

Brand extensions have led to fashion designers creating eyeglasses and sunglasses, perfumes, watches, handbags, and all kinds of other products that are lifestyle signifiers. It is now possible for men and women to wear designer eyeglasses, sunglasses, shirts, pants, blouses, dresses, ties, scarves, underwear, shoes, stockings, watches, wallets, handbags, travel bags, perfumes, and fragrances all made by one fashion brand (though for some items one might need to buy something from a different brand because the brand extension is not complete). One problem with brand extension is that it may weaken the value of the brand by spreading it too thin—so thin that it loses its cachet.

When I taught courses on popular culture, I used to have my students keep journals in which they would analyze various texts, such as popular songs, films, television shows, and commercials. One of my students spent a great deal of time talking about his Polo clothes. He was proud of having so many Polo shirts and

---

Although fashion brands are large industries, they do not rank high in lists of important global brands. The top ten global brands in 2008, according to *Business Week*, were:

1. Coca-Cola	6. Toyota
2. IBM	7. Intel
3. Microsoft	8. McDonald's
4. General Electric	9. Disney
5. Nokia	10. Google

The highest ranking fashion house on the list was Louis Vuitton, at sixteenth place. Chanel was 60, Hermes 76, and Prada was 91 on the list of the top 100 global brands. Vuitton's worth was estimated at $21 billion, so it is a very large company, though small compared to Coca-Cola, valued at $66 billion.

Figure 4.8 Top Ten Global Brands

pants and spent a great deal of time writing about them. He also wrote about other aspects of consumer culture, denigrating a friend of his who purchased "entry-level" watches and automobiles (figure 4.8).

What Prada, Burberry, Ermenegildo Zegna, Louis Vuitton, Giorgio Armani, Salvatore Ferragamo, Dior, YSL, Ralph Lauren, Hilfiger, Hugo Boss, and other global fashion houses provide is a "look" that appeals to various individuals, and in many cases logos that show they could afford these expensive products. In his book, *Media Semiotics*, Marcel Danesi explains the importance of brands to people who purchase them. He points out that brands function at two levels. At the denotative level, a brand indicates a particular product. But brands function mostly at the connotative level. He writes (2002:186):

> Clearly, in the fashion industry, designer names such as Gucci, Armani, and Calvin Klein evoke images of *objets d'art*, rather than images of mere clothes, shoes, or jewellery; so too do names such as Ferrari, Lamborghini, and Maserati in the realm of automobiles. The manufacturer's name, in such cases, *extends* the denotative meaning of the product considerably. This extensional process is known, of course, as connotation. The signification system created to ensconce product image into the social mindset is a *de facto* connotative one. When people buy an Armani or a Gucci product, for instance, they feel that they are buying a work of art to be displayed on the body; when they buy Poison by Christian Dior, they sense they are buying a dangerous, but alluring, love potions... "No-name" products do not engender such mysterious connotations.

It is the connotations of the brands, the meanings generated—stylish, expensive, tasteful, and so on—that are critical and that bestow psychological payoffs and gratifications on those who wear designer clothes and other products.

We can describe objects such as watches, cell phones, MP3 players, pouches, handbags, and earrings as "lifestyle" props that we use to generate certain desired impressions in those with whom we come in contact. They are similar in nature to theatrical props that generate certain impressions in audiences of plays and movies. Earrings in our noses, lips, or tongues convey different impressions than do earrings placed in our ears, though which ear a man chooses to wear an earring conveys sexual preferences. A baseball cap with the brim on the back is different from a baseball cap with the brim on the front and suggests a different attitude toward authority.

These lifestyle objects generally convey their brand identity through their designs and through logos that are placed strategically on the objects; that is, where they can be easily seen. Logos can take many forms, such as symbols or pictographs, tied to the brand by advertising and initials (think, for example, of YSL). In some case the name of the brand is written out. The important thing for the user of these objects is that they be recognized so the brand is recognized by others.

Style and the Postmodern Problematic

There are many conflicting definitions of postmodernism and explanations of what it is and what its impact has been. One of the most commonly used definitions of postmodernism comes from the work of a French scholar, Jean-François Lyotard, who explained in his book *The Postmodern Condition: A Report on Knowledge* (xxiii, xxiv):

> The object of this study is the condition of knowledge in the most highly developed societies. I have decided to use the word *postmodern* to describe that condition...I will use the term *modern* to designate any science that legitimates itself with reference to metadiscourse...making an explicit appeal to some grand narrative...If a metanarratives implying a philosophy of history is used to legitimate knowledge, questions

are raised concerned the validity of the institutions governing the social bond; these must be legitimated as well. Thus, justice is consigned to the grand narrative in the same way as truth.

Simplifying to the extreme, I define *postmodernism* as incredulity toward metanarratives.

Metanarratives are the old overarching philosophical systems that philosophers and others used to explain the way society works, such as a belief in progress and in social justice.

When these grand metanarratives were cast off, people were left to their own devices and needed to create their own personal narratives. Postmodernism involves a break in differentiation, sometimes called "de-differentiation," and thus postmodernists didn't see radical differences between popular culture and elite culture, and adopted the pastiche—an art form made of bits and pieces of different things—as a representative art form.

Lyotard offers us a portrait of a postmodern lifestyle (1984:76)

Eclecticism is the degree zero of contemporary culture: one listens to reggae, watches a western, eats McDonald's food for lunch and local cuisine for dinner, wears Paris perfume in Tokyo and "retro" clothes in Hong Kong; knowledge is a matter for TV games. It is easy to find a public for eclectic works. By becoming kitsch, art panders to the confusion which reigns in the "taste" of the patrons. Artists, gallery owners, critics, and public wallow together in the "anything goes" and the epoch is one of slackening.

In postmodernist societies, people can be very eclectic in their tastes and mix together upscale branded products and generic ones, creating their own personal style or what some might regard as style confusion or stylelessness. One thing that this stylelessness does is enable us to mask our social status. People in postmodern societies are continually reinventing themselves and changing their identities, and since this is done through clothes and props, it means people must keep on consuming. Mass consumption, along with fascination with mass media and cell phones, MP3 players (such as iPods), and other items connected to communications, is considered to be one of the hallmarks of postmodern societies.

It is worth noting that when President Barack Obama visited the Queen of England, he gave her an iPod filled with show tunes and videos of a trip she made to the United States, so the Queen, an elderly lady who lives in a luxurious castle and who has a taste for horses, now is wired, just like millions of her subjects

CHAPTER 5

The Objects of Our Affection

The Middle Ages never forgot that all things would be absurd, if their meaning were exhausted in their function and their place in the phenomenal world, if by their essence they did not reach into a world beyond this. This idea of a deeper significance in ordinary things is familiar to us as well, independently of religious convictions: as an indefinite feeling which may be called up at any moment, by the sound of raindrops on the leaves or by the lamplight on the table... Here, then is the psychological foundation from which symbolism arises. So the conviction of a transcendental meaning in all things seeks to formulate itself. About the figure of the Divinity a majestic system of correlated figures crystallizes, which all have reference to Him, because all things derive their meaning from Him. The world unfolds itself like a vast whole of symbols, like a cathedral of ideas.

Johan Huizinga, *The Waning of the Middle Ages*

We might point out here... that there is virtually never an object for *nothing*... The paradox I want to point out is that these objects which always have, in principle, a function, a utility, a purpose, we believe we experience as pure instruments, whereas in reality they carry other things, they are also something else: they function as the vehicle of meaning: in other words, the object effectively serves some purpose, but it also serves to communicate information; we might sum it up by saying that there is always a meaning which overflows the object's use.

Roland Barthes, "Semantics of the Object,"
The Semiotic Challenge

I n this chapter I discuss a number of artifacts that play an important role in our everyday lives, what I call the objects of our affection. These objects are imbedded in our lives and reflect, in various ways, ideas we have about these objects and how they should look, how they should function, and the role they should play in our lives. In the first chapter of Harvey Moloch's *Where Stuff Comes From: How Toasters, Toilets, Cars, Computers, and Many Other Things Come to Be As They Are*, he writes (2003:1):

Where does it come from, this vast blanket of things—coffeepots and laptops, window fittings, lamps and fence finials, cars, hat pins, and hand trucks—that make up economies, mobilize desire, and so stir up controversy? The questions leads to others because nothing stands alone—to understand any one thing you have to learn how it fits into larger arrays of physical objects, social sentiments, and ways of being. In the world of goods, as in worlds of any other sort, each element in just one interdependent fragment of a larger whole.

We must realize that every product was designed, built, financed, and marketed by many people, so objects are only the tip of the iceberg. Behind every object there are usually teams of artists, designers, engineers, and others who are responsible for bringing the object into existence, whether it is an MP3 player, a pair of running shoes, or a package of cereal.

In the preceding chapter I focused on the way brands of products are used by people to create an identity for themselves, and I pointed out that in postmodern societies, people are often changing their identities. This means they must continually change such things as their hairstyle, hair color, clothes, and fragrances. My focus now is not on the relationship between brands and identity but on the social, psychoanalytic, economic, and cultural significance of the objects I deal with, objects that play an important role in our everyday lives in consumer cultures. I will begin each section of this chapter with a short quotation that is relevant to my discussion of the topic, except in the selections that I have taken from my own writings. What follows is an analytical cultural studies "shuffle" that focuses on our foods and various objects that play an important role in contemporary consumer cultures.

Coffee

Fernand Braudel
The Structures of Everyday Life: Civilization and Capitalism 15th–18th Century The Limits of the Possible.
New York: Harper & Row (1981:256–257)

The coffee shrub was once thought to be a native of Persia but more probably came from Ethiopia. In any case coffee shrub and coffee scarcely appeared before 1470. Coffee was being drunk in Aden at that date. It had reached Mecca by 1511 since in that year its consumption was forbidden there; the prohibition was repeated in 1524. It is recorded in Cairo in 1501 and Istanbul in 1517; after this it was forbidden and re-authorized at regular intervals. Meanwhile, it spread widely within the Turkish Empire, to Damascus, Aleppo (1532) and Algiers. By the end of the century, it had installed itself virtually throughout the Muslim world—though it was still rare in the Islamic regions of India....

It was certainly in Islam that coffee was first encountered by such Western travellers as Prospero Alpini, an Italian doctor, who stayed in Egypt in about 1590, or the swaggering Pietro della Valle, who was in Constantinople in 1615....A treatise on the *Usage du caphe, du the et du chocolate*, which appeared anonymously in Lyon in 1671 (and may have been by Jacob Spon), listed all the virtues attributed to the new drink:

> It dries up all cold and damp humours, drives away wind, strengthens the liver, relives dropsies by its purifying quality; sovereign equally for scabies and impurity of the blood, it revives the heart and its vital beat, relives those who have a cold in the head ...
>
> However, other doctors, and public rumour, claimed that coffee was an anti-aphrodisiac and a "eunuch's drink."

As a result of this publicity and despite these accusations, coffee made ground in Paris. Pedlars appeared on the scene during the last year of the seventeenth century...who carried trays in front of them with coffee pot, lighted stove and cups.

* * *

In recent years our consumption of coffee in America has risen considerably. In the 1980s coffee consumption had fallen a great deal and something like fifty percent of Americans over ten years of age did not drink coffee, as more and more people started drinking soft drinks. It was around then that the specialty coffee market started developing, and Starbucks coffee started its march to colonize America. In her book *Brands*, Celia Lury describes the strategy that Starbucks employed. She writes (2004:28):

> The aim of the soon-to-be Starbucks CEO Howard Schulz was to transform coffee from a commodity ("something

to be bagged and sent home with the groceries") into a branded offering that consumers associated with (consistent) quality, service and community.

There are almost 12,000 Starbucks coffee shops in the United States as I write this, and who knows how many there will be when this book is published. During the economic malaise of recent years, Starbucks closed some of its stores, but when the economy rebounds, Starbucks will probably continue to open new stores. Starbucks has a policy of clustering its stores so the brand will attract attention and deter other coffee shops, even though there is a cost of cannibalization to be paid for this policy. Every time you turn around, a new Starbucks appears, or so it seems. In addition to Starbucks and those competing with it are countless other cafes, restaurants, and donut and coffee shops that sell coffee, of one kind or another.

There are more than 100 Starbucks coffee shops in Seattle, but small coffeehouses are able to compete with Starbuck there, according to an article "Smaller houses thrive in Starbucks' Shadow" by Allison Linn in the September 11, 2006 issue of the *San Francisco Examiner*. What Starbucks did was convince the American public that it was acceptable to pay up to $5.00 for a cup of coffee. That helped the smaller specialty coffeehouses. Starbuck's provides mass-produced coffees and cannot offer the kinds of coffees one finds at various "new-wave" and very upscale coffeehouses.

According to an article by Peter Meehan in *The New York Times*, "Brewing for the True Believer: Espresso's New Wave Hits Town" (Sept. 13, 2006: D1,D5), these new and very serious (about coffee) coffeehouses take infinite pains with every aspect of making coffee. This involves freshly roasting high-quality beans, grinding the coffee beans just before the coffee is to be used, steaming milk separately for each cup of coffee, paying attention to the fineness of the grind, heating the water to the exact temperature desired, giving the right dose (amount of coffee used for each cup), and tamping it correctly. The current commercial espresso maker of choice for the new-wave baristas is a $9,500 machine, the Cyncra, made by a company named Synesso in Seattle.

These new "artisinal" coffee shops use around 20 grams for each 1.5–2.5 ounce shot of espresso, much more than the typical 7 grams per ounce of espresso that is the industry standard. By taking infinite pains, the baristas make coffee with very flavorful terra-cotta colored cremas that are long lasting and very rich, because the oils and sugars in the coffee beans have been emulsified properly. The coffee at these coffeehouses is not like what you find in Starbucks, where the coffee machines are semiautomatic, the coffee beans are roasted in huge quantities, and there is little control that the baristas have over the final product.

I started drinking espresso coffee in Italy in 1963. I was living in Milan and teaching at the University of Milan. I purchased a small stove-top Bialetti espresso maker and, what was most important, wonderful and very rich Italian espresso coffee beans. Even then good espresso coffee was expensive. I now use a small Krups electric espresso maker, which creates decent coffee, but there is no crema and it cannot compare to coffee made with powerful espresso machines.

Dunkin' Donuts, which is much more downscale than Starbucks and located mostly in the eastern part of the United States, has 5,000 outlets and is hoping to have as many as 15,000 by 2020, according to an article in the September 18, 2006 issue of *Fortune* magazine. It is remodeling many of its restaurants to move a bit more upscale to what has been described as "blue-collar chic." Many of the Dunkin' Donut franchises now also sell espresso-based coffee drinks. Currently Dunkin' Donuts has eighteen percent of the coffee drink share in American restaurants. It competes mostly with chains like McDonald's and Burger King, which now are paying more attention to their coffee sales, since coffee is a product with large profit margins. Dunkin' Donuts makes much more profit from selling coffee than from its donuts.

What Starbucks did was to bring European-style espresso coffee drinks to the general public in America. Espresso and various coffee drinks made from espresso—cappuccinos and lattes and their variations—have always been available in Italian cafes and restaurants and in some of the larger cities in the United States, but was not part of mainstream coffee drinking here until the Starbucks era. Espresso coffee is much richer, more complex, and more flavorful than typical American (percolator or drip-grind) coffee. The espresso machines pressure hot water through finely ground coffee to extract the richness found in espresso coffee. But you need expensive, high-quality coffee and powerful espresso machines to get cremas and the flavor people like.

Starbucks also provides is a simulation of the typical European coffeehouse, where people can read newspapers and socialize in surroundings that are pleasant, and at times even elegant. There are a number of Starbucks coffeehouses in Mill Valley, where I reside. I often meet friends in one of them near my house, where we can relax and chat with no pressure on us to drink our coffee and leave. This particular Starbucks has some nice large stuffed chairs and a sofa in addition to wooden chairs and formica tables. Starbucks is a meeting place for many people who find it a convenient place to get together with friends.

One of the notions most strongly associated with coffee is sociability and relaxation. Coffee is a drink that we associate with conversations and community, so there are psychological benefits to drinking coffee, especially in pleasant surroundings. The latest findings by scientists studying coffee drinking suggest that it is beneficial for people if drunk in moderation. So coffee, even when it is of mediocre quality, can be doubly good for us—helping us connect to others and helping our bodies fight off illnesses.

But this is not the case for all coffee—or, more precisely, certainly not coffee-based drinks. The Center for Science in the Public Interest provides information about the calories in some coffees as shown in figure 5.1 (adapted from Marian Burros'

Coffee	Calories	Equivalent To
Starbucks Venti (20 oz.)	490	Quarter-Pounder with cheese
Java chip 24 oz. Frappucino with whipped cream	650	McDonald's coffee, 11 creamers, and 29 packets of sugar

Figure 5.1 Calories in Some Coffee Drinks

"Eating Well Notebook," *New York Times*, September 13, 2006:D5).

We see, then, that some coffee drinks are not good for you, since these drinks are full of fat and calories. A Java chip Frappucino with whipped cream contains approximately an entire day's allowance of saturated fat. Coffee becomes a culinary Trojan horse full of sugar and saturated fat. The moral of this disquisition is—if you like coffee, drink coffee, but keep away from coffee-flavored drinks.

The recession of 2008 and 2009 led to Americans changing their coffee drinking habits in major ways and Starbucks had to close hundreds of its stores. During this period, the $4.00 cup of coffee lost much of its appeal; in addition, Starbucks also had made changes to its store that deleted its cachet. As I write, it is trying to regain its appeal and is now selling a bargain cup of coffee and breakfast for $3.95. Whether Americans will return to purchasing expensive coffee when the recession is over remains to be seen.

The Toaster

Arthur Asa Berger
Bloom's Morning: Coffee, Comforters, and the Secret Meaning of Everyday Life
Boulder, CO: Westview Press (1997:155–158)

The existence of the toaster implies the existence of sliced bread. For that is what one uses in a toaster. And sliced bread, itself, implies a certain kind of bread: bread that has a particular form or shape most practical for slicing. Bread has been mechanized and standardized and is no longer a product with an irregular shape; it no longer need be touched by human hands.

This does not mean that we do not have other kinds of bread. We do, but generally they cost more than the standard loaf of white or whole-grain bread. These "touched by human hands" breads tend to be ethnic—French, Italian, Jewish, Russian—and are generally slightly irregular in shape, often having a crust.

The toaster is part of a system and only has significance relative to the wrapped, pan-made, thin-crusted bread that can be used in it. One problem with this bread is that it is very soft and spongy. This is the result of the mechanization of bread, described by Sigfried Giedion in *Mechanization Takes Command* as follows (1969:193):

> The bread of full mechanization has the resiliency of a rubber sponge. When squeezed it returns to its former shape. The loaf becomes constantly whiter, more elastic, and frothier...Since mechanization, it has often been pointed out, white bread has become much richer in fats, milk, and sugar. But these are added largely to stimulate sales by heightening the loaf's eye-appeal. The shortenings used in bread, a leading authority states, are "primarily for the purpose of imparting desirable tender eating or chewing qualities to the finished product." They produce the "soft velvet crumb," a cake-like structure, so that the bread is half-masticated, as it were, before reaching the mouth.

Giedion has also described this bread as neither bread nor cake but something halfway between the two. This kind of bread is a highly rationalized product designed to maximize profit for the baker. The consumers had to be "taught" to like this kind of bread, and it was, no doubt, part of the process of "Americanization" that many ethnic groups underwent, a way of repudiating one's ethnic identity and non-American-ness.

(There are, of course, new developments taking place. In large cities one can get "handbaked" breads that are more substantial and more interesting. And even packaged bread seems to be changing, so that more whole-grain breads are available as alternatives to the standard loaf of white bread.) One thing the toaster does is change the nature of this bread, giving it a color, making it firmer and easier to handle.

An interesting philosophical problem is raised by the toaster. What is toast—the product of a process or the process itself? That is, does bread become toast (and change its identity somehow) or do we toast bread and thereby only modify its character slightly? Is toast bread that has been processed (toasted) or changed (made into toast)?

Obviously we start off with a piece of bread—and for our purposes, let us assume that we have the standard loaf of sliced pan bread with its thin crust. The question is whether we end up with a variation of the piece of sliced bread or something that is different. In terms of the dynamics of American culture, I would suggest that we would like to think that toast is something different from bread, per se. That is, the process involves a major transformation (in the same way that grinding a steak turns it into hamburger). We believe in the power of change and in our ability to change our circumstance and status.

This kind of white bread may be the perfect product for the middle classes, standing midway, as they do, between the upper-classes and the working-classes. Their bread, if Giedion is right, is midway between traditional bread and cake (neither one nor the other). Toast may suggest, unconsciously, a transformation to a higher status. The working classes eat their crusts of bread; the elites "take toast and tea."

The toaster has also led to the development of new products, the most pernicious of which is probably the "pop tart," meant to be "baked" in the toaster as a mechanized kind of sweet roll. The pop tart is a new food product and a relatively successful one, though its sweetness makes it appealing mostly to young children. Toasters themselves have undergone transformations. Older versions required the person making the toast to flip the toast over when one side was done. The toast had to be watched. Then came the "pop" toaster, which toasts bread to whatever degree of lightness or darkness one wants, then pops it up. In the earlier versions of the pop toaster one had to depress the bread using some kind of knob or lever, but the most advanced form of toaster now has a mechanism that takes care of that. One merely inserts the bread in the opening in the toaster and it sinks slowly out of sight, to reemerge, almost magically, when it has become toast.

For large families there are toasters that can toast four slices of bread at a time to different degrees of darkness. Thus a toaster can be spewing out light, medium, and dark toast more or less at the same time. Heat sensors in the toaster measure the temperature and the moisture content of the bread and pop it up at the proper moment. (Making toast on the basis of timers is old-fashioned and low-tech.)

Ultimately the toaster is an apology for the quality of our bread. It attempts, heroically, to transform the semisweet, characterless, "plastic" packaged bread that we have learned to love into something more palatable and more manageable. Perhaps our handling this bread and warming it up gives us a sense that the bread now has a human touch to it, is not an abstract, almost unreal product. The toaster represents a heroic attempt to redeem our packaged bread, to redeem the unredeemable. But the toaster, despite its high-tech functions, is doomed to the continual repetition of (symbolically speaking) Adam and Eve's Fall, for an unregenerate bread cannot be saved.

Every piece of toast is a tragedy.

* * *

Note: A selection from this chapter was republished by *Harper's* a number of years ago and the book from which this chapter was taken, *Bloom's Morning*, has been translated into German and Chinese. I own the copyright for this book.

Swaddling Cloths

Geoffrey Gorer and John Rickman
The People of Great Russia: A Psychological Study
New York: W.W. Norton (1962:97–98, 123–124)

From the day of its birth onward the baby is tightly swaddled in long strips of material, holding its legs straight and arms down by its sides. When Russians are asked why they swaddle their babies in this way, they give a considerable variety of reasons, but they all have one common theme: the baby is potentially so strong that if it were not swaddled it would risk destroying itself or doing itself irreparable harm, and would be impossible to handle...All Russians are agreed that an unswaddled baby is impossible to handle, and would jump out of constraining arms; Russians exposed to Occidental practices justified swaddling on the ground that Russians had no perambulators.

When swaddled the baby is completely rigid; one informant said the infants were like sticks, another likened them to sausages, a third to parcels. The baby can be held in any position and by any part of it without bending, and temporarily unswaddled infants are...liable to maintain rigid poses which are very unusual in Occidental babies ....

The deductions which follow are unverified hypotheses, though verification could be obtained...When human infants are not constrained, they move their limbs and bodies a great deal, especially during the second six months of life...While they are swaddled in the Russian manner, Russian infants can do none of these things; and it is assumed that Russian infants can do none of these things; and it is assumed that this inhibition of movement is felt to be extremely painful and frustrating and is responded to with intense and destructive rage, which cannot be adequately expressed physically. This rage, it is assumed, is directed at the constraint rather than at the people who constrain the infant.

* * *

Geoffrey Gorer and John Rickman's book *The People of Great Russia* advances a hypothesis—and Gorer takes pains to point out that it is a hypothesis—that the practice of the great Russians in swaddling their children helped explain certain aspects of Russian personality and character. Swaddling babies led, he suggested, to a destructive rage in Russian babies and to extreme behavior when they grew up. They either cowed cravenly before authority or lorded over those beneath them in an extremely authoritarian manner; they alternated between starving and orgiastic feasts. In all cases, their extreme behavior was shaped, Gorer suggests, by their earliest experiences of being tied up and confined by swaddling clothes when they were babies and not able to move their arms and legs and explore the world the way babies do in other countries. Some Russian informants told me that they used swaddling clothes on their children and that many Russian parents continue to use swaddling clothes.

This hypothesis might help explain the kind of bizarre and extreme characters one finds in Dostoevsky's novels and in many other Russian literary works. Works of fiction generally reflect the dominant codes and values and beliefs found in a culture, which is why literary works can be analyzed to help understand the societies and cultures in which they are created.

Gorer's thesis is that all of our physical and cultural needs and desires are shaped, one way or another, by our cultures, and the way we are treated when we are children plays an important role in the way we act when we are grown up. Our earliest experiences shape, but don't completely determine, our behavior when we are older. The child, in many respects, is the father of the man and the woman. We never stop learning, Gorer writes, but earlier experiences are more powerful than later ones.

Every society is different, which means that members of these societies (and the various subcultures in them) have different ideas about how to raise children. Some, like the Great Russians Gorer writes about, used to wrap them up in swaddling cloths while others, making sure they don't hurt themselves, let them do anything they want. The logic of the swaddling cloths suggests a society filled with either anarchists (the baby is let free, finally, and wants everyone else to be free) or totalitarian despots (who want to constrain everyone else the way they were once constrained).

There is a curious practice in Bali that is of interest here. Because of religious prohibitions, the Balinese do not allow their babies to touch the ground until they are 210 days old, which is approximately seven months using a standard calendar. Balinese babies are carried around by their mothers, brothers, sisters, and relatives until they are one year old in the Balinese calendar. They are not swaddled but they are "confined" in a sense. Yet this practice does not seem to have a negative impact on the babies, and may in fact make them feel a great deal more secure and more attached to their parents and siblings.

In Hedrick Smith's book *The Russians*, his description of Russian feasting calls to mind Gorer's swaddling clothes hypothesis and its impact—which explains why the Russians move between extremes in an almost bipolar manner. Hedrick remarks how Russians are always looking for occasions to have a party, often spend an entire bonus on a feast, and he adds that Russians are not, by nature, moderate or frugal. They crave was they call "*lyuks*," luxury, Hedrick says, which they experience when they are feasting and drinking to excess. They switch back and forth, it seems, between feast and meager repasts. They often pool their money to have elaborate parties in someone's apartment, where they have orgiastic feasts and wild drinking parties. In these parties, vodka plays an all-important role.

The "Evangelical" Hamburger

Arthur Asa Berger
The Minnesota Daily (1965)

McDonald's offers the hamburger without qualities for the man without qualities. It must be seen as more than a gaudy, vulgar oasis of tasteless ground meat, a fountain of sweet, syrupy malted milks in a big parking lots that caters to insolvent students, snack seekers, and hard-up hungers who grind its bloody gristle through their choppers at fifteen cents a shot. No! McDonalds is not just a hamburger joint...it is America, or, rather, it is the supreme triumph of all that is insane in American life.

At McDonald's there is no human touch...just little packets of wrapped hamburgers, sacks of fried potatoes—everything is packed in little bags to be thrown away. Is there any pleasure connected with eating a McDonald hamburger? I think not! The only relief you have is that it didn't cost sixteen cents or even twenty cents. It only costs fifteen cents because American technology and free enterprise have dictated that an automated hamburger is worth only fifteen cents, and any corporation that takes the joy out of eating a lowly hamburger, that pushes its crass utilitarianism down our throats must only charge fifteen cents. It is almost a moral law that the great McDonald cannot violate.

But we purchase our McDonald's hamburger at great cost. We cannot have it rare or well done, we cannot have it without "the works" for that would destroy the genius of the McDonald hamburger. No! WE get the great national hamburger—prepared to hamburgize the masses—which forces us to sacrifice our individuality, our gastronomic identity, for a few pennies. Instead of a hamburger being prepared for our tastes, we are forced to adapt ourselves to it; we must become, so to speak, molded to its taste. The triumph of McDonaldism is the death of individualism and the eating of a McDonald's hamburger is the next thing to a death wish.

A McDonald's hamburger reminds you how very mortal you are, how you too will be thrown away someday in the moral equivalent of a paper bag.

* * *

I wrote this essay, published in *The Minnesota Daily* in 1965, under the title "The Evangelical Hamburger," full of purple prose and dire warnings. I wrote it after I had eaten my first McDonald's hamburger. There had been an empty lot I often passed when walking to my office at the University of Minnesota, where I taught courses in English composition and literature (while I was in graduate school working on my Ph.D. degree). One day when I passed the lot I saw a small, white building with huge yellow arches and an electronic sign, full of rapidly rising numbers, indicating the number of people who had eaten McDonald's hamburgers. It struck me that the arches had a religious significance to them and the electronic sign indicated that people who ate a McDonald's hamburger were members of a community, or, even stronger, a congregation. And the way one ordered a hamburger seemed very structured or, in effect, a ritual. The fifteen cents could be construed as an offering to the new religion. I recognized then that McDonald's would spread, with "evangelical" fervor, all through America and the world. The McDonald's hamburger, only fifteen cents in 1963, was for me a symbol of the forces of mechanization and standardization that I felt were to dominate American culture and society.

There are now, according to an article by Janet Adamy in *The Wall Street Journal*, around 13,500 McDonald's hamburger joints and countless Burger Kings, KFCs, and other fast food emporia in the United States. There are, it turns out, 20,000 Subway outlets in America, and in 1999 there was one fast food restaurant for every 196 households in the United States ("For Subway, Every Nook and Cranny on the Planet is Possible Site for a Franchise," September 11, 2006:A11). According to another article by Gordon Fairclough and Janet Adamy in *The Wall Street*

Journal, "Sex, Skin, Fireworks, Licked Fingers—It's a Quarter Pounder Ad in China" (September 21, 2006) McDonald's in China is making "steamy" print advertisements and even steamier television commercials linking beef to manliness, luxuriousness, and sexiness. By 2008, McDonald's expected to have 1,000 stores in China, 230 more than it had in 2006.

There seems to be good reason to suspect that the growth of these fast food restaurants, with their fat-filled products, have contributed in some measure to the epidemic of obesity in the United States and elsewhere in the world. Obesity now is a problem in China, India, and many other third-world countries. Two-thirds of Americans are now considered overweight or obese. Obesity leads to many serious diseases, such as heart trouble and diabetes, which greatly increase the cost of medical care. Diabetes is now epidemic in the United States and a number of other countries. It is a very serious disease because it triggers so many other life-threatening illnesses.

I can recall hearing a news program recently in which a doctor pointed out that because of all the fast food they eat, the veins and arteries of many adolescents now are similar to those of people in their fifties and sixties. Thus, ironically, Americans (and people in other countries) who frequently patronize fast food restaurants may save some money on hamburgers, French fries, and other kinds of fast foods, but they end up spending a great deal more money on medical care for ailments generated by their being overweight and, in many cases, obese. And those of us who do not eat fast foods end up paying increased taxes that are needed to pay for expensive medical care for overweight and obese people. So there are major social, political, and economic considerations tied to every bite a person takes of a McDonald's hamburger.

French-Fried Potatoes

Eric Schlosser
Fast Food Nation: The Dark Side of the All-American Meal
New York: Perennial (2005:114–115)

The success of Richard and Mac McDonald's hamburger stand had been based as much on the quality of their fries as on the taste of their burgers. The McDonald brothers had devised an elaborate system for making crisp french fries, one that was later improved by the restaurant chain. McDonald's cooked thinly sliced Russet Burbanks in a special fryer to keep oil temperature above 325 degrees. As the chain expanded, it became more difficult—and yet all the more important—to maintain the consistency and quality of the fries. J.R. Simplot met with Ray Kroc in 1965. The idea of switching to frozen french fries appealed to Kroc, as a means of ensuring the quality and cutting labor costs. McDonald's obtained its fresh potatoes from about 175 different local suppliers, and crew members spent a great deal of time peeling and slicing potatoes. Simplot offered to build a new factory solely for the manufacture of McDonald's french fries. Kroc agrees to try Simplot's fries but made no long-term commitment. The deal was sealed with a handshake.

McDonald's began to sell J.R. Simplot's frozen french fries the following year. Customers didn't notice any difference in taste. And the reduced cost of using a frozen product made french fries one of the most profitable items on the menu— far more profitable than hamburgers. Simplot quickly became the main supplier of French fries to McDonald's. At the time McDonald's had about 725 restaurants in the United States. Within a decade it had 3000. Simplot sold his frozen french fries to other restaurant chains, accelerating the growth of the fast food industry.

*   *   *

Schlosser provides some interesting statistical information about McDonald's French fries, which, it turns out, are more profitable than their hamburgers. These figures deal with per capita consumption of potatoes in the United States (figure 5.2).

Date	Fresh Potato Consumption	French Fries Consumption
1960	81 pounds	4 pounds
2000	49 pounds	30 pounds

Figure 5.2   Consumption of French-Fried Potatoes in the United States

We are now eating, on average, almost eight times as many French-fried potatoes as we did in 1960. McDonald's changed the oil it used from a beef-tallow-dominated oil to a pure vegetable oil, but still there are protests from nutritional watchdog groups about the quality of the oil used by McDonald's and other fast food emporia, and it is investigating changing to an oil with no transfats. Some chains have already made the change.

Americans purchase some ninety percent of these French fries at fast food restaurants; French fries, Schlosser explains, are now the most widely sold cooked food product in the country. Part of this may be because women who work don't want to bother cooking French fries at home, and many young women hardly cook at all, regardless of their marital status. Because fries are very high in calories and full of fat, they most certainly are a major contributor to the epidemic of obesity in this country, and now, it turns out, all over the world.

There was a bizarre situation in the United States Congress that took place when the French government refused to go along with the American government over invading Iraq. Some irate Republican congressmen insisted that we change French fries to "Freedom fries," and this absurdity lasted a couple of years.

A friend of mine who was in the marketing business was retained by a competitor of McDonald's to find out why it was so popular. Research by my friend's company revealed that people liked burgers from Burger King better than McDonald's burgers, but liked the McDonald's French fries the best. If one is a fast food hamburger and fries aficionado, the best of all possible worlds would be getting a burger at Burger King and fries at McDonald's.

By a curious coincidence, in 1965, when I wrote my article about McDonald's having the hallmarks of an evangelical religion, Ray Kroc was meeting with J. R. Simplot. The era of the frozen McDonald's French fries and the global spread of McDonald's hamburger restaurants and others like it was about to begin.

Fountain Pens and Ink

Asa Briggs
Victorian Things
London: B. T. Batsford (1988:186–187)

"Fountain pens" of all colours, shapes and sizes were being widely advertised during the late-Victorian years: they bore familiar names like "Swan" and "Waterman." Surprisingly, although the thing—a fountain pen—was new, the word was not: the *New Oxford Dictionary* gives the date 1710 for the first use of the expression "fountain ink horns or fountain pens." It was not until 1835, however, that John Joseph Parker, another of the still familiar names in the pen-making business, secured a patent for "certain improvements in fountain pens"—at that time they were more often called "reservoir pens"—which permitted self-filling. By the end of the reign you could usually buy a fountain pen for as little as 3d. There were even some which cost a penny.

Parker was only one, if the best-known, of a large number of inventors who discovered radically different ways of feeding the pen with ink. Increasingly the ink as well as the pen was trademarked. Ink of the quill pen was not suited for the steel pen; it corroded the nib, and Henry Stephens chose the right moment to set us his first ink factory in 1834. Very soon "Stephens' ink" became the best known of all inks, with Waterman's coming second. Stephens' ink was advertised grandiloquently at first as "a carbonaceous black writing fluid which will accomplish the so-long desired and apparently hopeless task of rendering the manuscript as durable and indelible as the printed record." Yet soon it became a household necessity. Meanwhile, aniline dyes changed the composition of ink which could be sold also in the form not of fluids but powders, and it was these that were used by the new School Boards after 1870 in order to save money.

*   *   *

What struck me, when I read this selection, was how some of the companies Briggs mentions—Waterman and Parker—are still making fountain pens and ink. Certain fountain pens are now thought of as art objects and there are large numbers of people who collect them. Some fountain pens, with gold nibs and jewels, cost a great deal of money: hundreds and even thousands of dollars. However, you can still get a serviceable Waterman's fountain pen for $35 or $40.

I've had a number of fountain pens over the years, including an "entry-level" Mont Blanc pen. One of my favorites was a Parker with a stainless steel body that I used for forty years for writing in my journals. It came with a lifetime guarantee, so if you had a problem with the nib, you could send it back to the factory and they would send you a new nib or a new pen.

Around 2006 I gave up on fountain pens—with the bother of having to fill them, with their clotting, with getting ink on my fingers, and started writing with black 0.5-mm rollerball pens from Office Depot. You can get a package of 36 of them for less than $10 when they are on sale. When I was still in my fountain pen stage, I used a Pelikan fountain pen India ink, which was always clotting, and so I found myself spending a good deal of time fiddling around with my fountain pen to get it to write. I chose the rollerball model because the line I get from the rollerball looks exactly like the line I got from my trusty Parker.

The fountain pen era ended for most people some sixty years ago with the development of ballpoint pens. In recent years, pen companies have come up with many different writing technologies, of which the rollerball is my personal favorite. When the sales were on for the start of the school year, drug stores and stationery stores were selling Bic and other ballpoint pens for just a few cents a pen. The world, we might say, is divided into two groups of pen users: the pragmatists, who use ballpoint pens or rollerball pens or some other similar new technology, and the aesthetes, who cling to their "old-fashioned" but in many cases very beautiful and very expensive fountain pens.

Bikinis

Frank A. Salamone
Popular Culture in the Fifties
Lanham, MD: University Press of America (2001:75–76)

The bikini was born in Paris in the forties. In 1946, the bikini [was] called the Atome. Its name was changed to commemorate the island on which the Atom Bomb was originally tested. It became famous when worn by fifties "love goddess" actresses such as Brigitte Bardot, Anita Ekberg and Sophia Loren. Most people, however, considered the bikini more appropriate to strip joints than public beaches. In fact, many European beaches banned the Bikini for years.

Surprisingly, the United States did not ban the Bikini officially, but it really did not catch on until about 1960. The popular song "Itsy Bitsy Teeny Weeny Yellow Polka Dot Bikini" gives a good idea of its risqué reputation. The song states that the wearer of it is "afraid to come out of the water: because she would embarrass herself. In fact, sociologists point out that there are mosaics from the fourth-century villa at Piazza America in Sicily which depict women wearing bikinis.

Indeed, even before the 1940s there were two piece bathing suits before the bikini. As part of the cutbacks due to the war, the American government in 1948 ordered a ten percent reduction in the fabric used in women's swimwear. The skirt panel and bare midriff were sacrificed. The original bikini, however, was but 30 inches of fabric, outdoing the wartime two-piece suit. The bikini was but a bra top and two triangles held together by a string—and a prayer. A woman's navel was actually on display...

In 1957 a magazine stated "It is hardly necessary to waste words over the so-called bikini since it is inconceivable that any girl with tact and decency would ever wear such a thing." Yet, in but a few years the bikini began to appear somewhat modest compared with other styles of the sixties.

*   *   *

It wasn't so many years ago that magazines airbrushed out women's navels. Now, in the era of the bare midriff, that seems quite fantastic. It is not unusual for young women now to display a goodly amount of their bodies, from just below their breasts to just above their pubic hair and vaginas. It seems, in the Britney Spears era, that young women "love goddesses" in America, and many other countries as well, seem to think that their hips, along with their breast cleavage, are powerful "turn-ons" for men. Even fleshy, and in some cases obese, young women have adopted this look. In some places in America, now, young women have taken to exposing their breasts and even stripping in public places.

We Americans are, of course, behind the times when it comes to women finding ways to expose their bodies to "the male gaze," as feminists describe it—a term used to describe the lustful way that women are gazed at by males as a means of expressing their power and dominance. In Brazil, most of the bikinis are so scant that when you see a woman wearing one there, almost nothing is left for one's imagination. And there are nude beaches in Europe, and now also in some beaches in America as well.

John Berger, in his book *Ways of Seeing*, explains that there is a difference between being nude and naked. As he writes in his discussion of European oil painting traditions (1972:54):

> To be naked is to be oneself.
>   To be nude is to be seen as naked by others and yet not recognized for oneself. A naked body has to been as an object in order to become a nude. (The sight of it as an object stimulates the use of it as an object.) Nakedness reveals itself. Nudity is placed on display.

The fact that young women put themselves on display is, many feminist theorists argue, a sign of male dominance in what has been described as a phallocentric or penis-centered culture.

One of the curious aspects of sexuality is that nude women are not as sexually exciting for men as partially dressed (and therefore partially undressed) women. Where one draws the line between the degree of being undressed or naked and of exposing some of one's breasts and other body parts to generate maximum sexual excitement and stimulation in males has yet to be found.

Vodka

Hedrick Smith
The Russians
New York: Quadrangle/The New York Times Book Co.
(1976:120–121)

The West has nothing equivalent to vodka, the way Russians drink it. Like corruption, vodka is one of the indispensable lubricants of Russian life. The mere mention of vodka starts Russians salivating and puts them in a mellow mood. It would take an encyclopedia to explain all the vodka lore from the gentle tap under the throat which signifies drinking to the scores of ditties Russians have invented to convey the message, "let's go drink." Vodka eases the tension of life. It helps people to get to know each other, for many a Russian will say that he cannot trust another man until they have drunk seriously together. Vodka-drinking is invested with the symbolism of machismo…Among working men and peasants, vodka is so popular that the $4.80 half-liter bottle is better than cash for odd jobs.

Those who have not been exposed to Russian drinking do not appreciate how hard Russians drink but travelers to Russia…have remarked about it for centuries. In 1639, Adam Orleans, who represented the Duke of Holstein's court in Moscow, observed that Russians "are more addicted to drunkenness than any nation in the world." In 1839, the Marquis de Custine, a French nobleman, picked up the Russian aphorism that "drinking is the joy of Russia." It still is, but this does not mean Russians are relaxed social imbibers. They know no moderation. Once the vodka bottle is uncorked, it must be finished…Russians drink essentially to obliterate themselves, to blot out the tedium of life, to warm themselves from the chilling winters, and they eagerly embrace the escapism it offers…Intoxication is the major factor in the majority of all crimes (90 percent of murders), accounts for more than half of all traffic accidents, figures in 63 percent of all accidental drownings …

* * *

In searching Google for data on vodka consumption in Russia, I came across a number of remarkable statistics. It is estimated that in Russia around 2000 AD, with a population of 146 million people, some 40,000 Russians died of alcohol poisoning, a rate of 27.5 percent per 100,000 people. In one article, it was estimated that 700,000 deaths a year are caused by alcohol abuse in Russia, and since vodka accounts for seventy-five percent of all distilled alcohol consumed, vodka is the main cause or certainly a major contributing factor behind these deaths.

Another article I found on the Internet stated that between 1960 and 1987, 30–35 million Russians died because of alcohol abuse. That would come to around one million Russians a year dying of alcohol abuse. Russians consume around four billion liters of alcoholic beverages a year, or fifteen liters of hard alcohol per capita. In 1980, vodka consumption of was 0.8 gallons per capita. By 1984 it was 3.75 gallons per capita. It has been estimated that one in seven adult Russians is an alcoholic and one third of Russian men binge drink once a month.

So vodka plays an important role in Russian society and culture, and its impact has been devastating from a public health point of view. The Russians do not sip vodka the way Americans do; the custom there is to drink it in one gulp—bottles up or "*pey dedna*," as the Russians put it. This kind of drinking would be in keeping with Gorer's notion, discussed earlier in this chapter, that the Great Russians, because they were swaddled and kept constrained when they were babies, behave excessively and erratically when they are free of the physical constraints and cultural codes that were used to bind them. Russia is part of a vodka belt that extends from the Scandinavian countries through Eastern Europe to Russia—a region where there is much alcohol abuse, though the amount of abuse varies from country to country. When I was in Finland one summer, it wasn't unusual to see drunks lying around on sidewalks at 10:00 a.m.

In the United States, vodka accounts for around twenty-five percent of all distilled spirits, but there is a more developed beer and wine culture here than in Russia, though beer consumption is rising now in Russia. But statistics on binge drinking in America are alarming, and although alcohol abuse and alcoholism isn't as big a problem in America as it is in Russia, it still is a major problem, and vodka, which accounts for a quarter of all our hard liquor, seems to be one of the main culprits.

Beer

R. Brasch
How Did It Begin?
New York: Pocket Books (1969:94–95)

Man began his modern drinking habits with the imbibing of beer, his oldest alcoholic drink. He did not invent its production but discovered it in the process of nature. Possibly some bread crumbs fell into water and started fermenting. Tasting the product, primitive man rather enjoyed it and long before the development of his scientific mind, started his own research. ...

The history of brewing goes back well over 10,000 years. It began long before the Egyptians had started building their first pyramid. It almost coincides with the first making of bread. Indeed, baking and brewing thus went together. ...

The brewing of beer was so sacred that, among some tribes, men engaged in the task were kept isolated from their womenfolk. Otherwise, it was believed, the magic transformation of Corn into Spirit would not take place.

One of the most ancient clay tablets in existence, dating back to the year 6000 B.C., depicts a crude type of beer-making for sacrificial purposes. By 4000 B.C. they had learnt to produce 16 different types of the beverage. Brewing was a privilege set aside for their kings and restricted to temples. Thus the earliest breweries were places of worship! ...

Its early religious association lingered on through the ages. Medieval monasteries excelled in making beer and provided different brands for the monks and their guests, each of whom was given a gallon a day.

Churches sold beer to raise funds. It became the most popular drink at weddings where it was poured by the bride herself. Thus it became known as the *bride's ale*, accounting for the word *bridal!*

Beer even made history. It was because their casks were almost empty that the Pilgrim Fathers, sailing on the *Mayflower,* decided to cut the voyage short and look for a port ahead of schedule....

* * *

It is possible to suggest that there are beer cultures and there are wine cultures. In most cultures, both beer and wine are available but in some cultures, beer dominates and in others wine dominates. A list of some of the more important beer and wine cultures in Europe is shown in figure 5.3.

We see that the wine cultures are Mediterranean ones, below the forty-ninth parallel for the most part, and the beer cultures tend to be northern and Atlantic ones, where grape vines do not grow as easily as in the wine countries. Beer was traditionally thought of as a drink for poor people or ordinary ones and wine for more affluent ones—a distinction that still has a degree of validity to it.

It's hard to classify the United States, because we drink a great deal of both beer and wine. Some countries, such as the Scandinavian and Slavic ones, seem to be what might be called "hard liquor" or "grain" liquor cultures—in which vodka and other hard drinks tend to be dominant. Of course, one way or another, people in just about every society find ways to make and drink alcoholic beverages, except in Muslim countries, where religion prohibits it. And many Muslims drink, too— but not in public.

It's interesting to know that human beings have been drinking beer and other alcoholic beverages for some 10,000 years.

Beer Cultures	Wine Cultures
England	France
Germany	Italy
Czech Republic	Spain
Belgium	Portugal

Figure 5.3 Beer Cultures and Wine Culture

Beer goes back a long way in human history. In the United States, the sales of the mass-produced beers such as Budweiser and Coors have been flat for a number of years, while the sales of microbreweries and what might be described as "gourmet" beers have been growing. Some big breweries now have their own microbrew beers. Light beer, which was originally introduced as a beer for women, failed when it was first introduced but then was repositioned, with the aid of beefy and "virile" football players and other athletes, into a mainstream drink for men and women.

A number of years ago a consortium of American beer companies ran a campaign to sell more beer here. Its slogan was "In this great land, beer belongs." And so it does, along with other staples of American culture, such as apple pie and ice cream, coffee, and Coca-Cola. In recent years beer has become increasingly popular in China, which has a long tradition of beer-making, with its excellent German-style Tsing Tao beer.

Veils

Marjorie Garber
Vested Interests: Cross-Dressing & Cultural Anxiety
New York: Harper (1992:338)

The veil is to clothing what the curtain is to the theater. It simultaneously reveals and conceals, marking a space of transgression and expectation; it leads the spectators to "fantasize about 'the real thing' in anticipation of seeing it."

The veil as a sign of the female or the feminine has a long history in Western culture, whether its context is religious chastity (the nun, the bride, the orthodox Muslim woman) or erotic play (the Dance of the Seven Veils). But presuppositions about the gendered function of the veil—that it is worn to mystify, to tantalize, to sacralize, to protect or to put out of bounds—are susceptible to cultural misprision as well as fetishization. Thus a German ethnologist who traveled for six months with the Tuareg of the North African desert felt called upon to report that there was "nothing effeminate about these Tuareg nobles...on the contrary, they are shrewd, ruthless men with a look of cold brutality in their eyes." Although the Tuareg were known as fierce warriors, the fact they their men wore veils at all times while Tuareg women freely showed their faces was clearly a puzzle. The men's eyes, however, were visible through a slit in the veil and could be construed, at least by those who expected or hoped to find such a thing, as showing "cold brutality"—in other words, manliness. This Eurocentric obsession with the veil as female—with what is veiled as woman—is established early in *Morocco* as itself a mystification and a coded sign.

At the beginning of the film Arab women unveil themselves flirtatiously at Gary Cooper from the tops of city buildings. On shipboard en route from Europe Dietrich wears a fashionable *Western* veil of sheer black netting...before making her appearance in male formal dress.

* * *

We do not think of veils as something men wear because of what might be called a "Eurocentric" perspective on things, yet as this selection points out, there are some places where men wear veils. And their eyes, in the case of the Tuareg men, reflect their "cold brutality," which is interpreted as a signifier of "manliness." These men are not effeminate, by any means. I have seen photographs of Zoroastrian men at a religious ceremony who are also wearing veils. So we are mistaken when we assume that veils are only worn by women.

Nevertheless, most people who wear veils are Muslim women; the practice is linked in our popular culture, as the film *Morocco* shows, with these Muslim women. If you were to visit Istanbul, you would see that most Muslim women there do not wear veils. You have to go to the "religious" cities in Turkey to find most of the women wearing veils. Veils have a double valence: they hide and they generate curiosity. Human being are, by nature, curious, so when a part of a woman's face is hidden, we cannot help but wonder what she really looks like. Because a veil covers most of a woman's face, her eyes become more significant.

It is reasonable to suggest that a veil, like a head scarf, is a signifier of religiosity in Muslim women, but many Muslim women do not wear either, especially those who live in big cities such as Istanbul and Marrakesh. In *The New York Times* September 8, 2006 edition (page A20), there is an article, "A Simple Scarf, But Meaning Much More Than Faith" about a young 21-year-old Muslim woman, Dena al-Atassi, who applied for a position in a Jenny Craig office in Florida and was turned down. Ms. Atassi decided to wear a head scarf when she turned sixteen. She alleges that the company turned her down because she is a Muslim and they want "all-American"-looking women. She spent three years in Syria and says that she noticed there that wearing a veil demonstrates a certain kind of self-confidence that she finds lacking in American women, who, she suggests, all want to look like Barbie dolls. The article points out that veils were once viewed as exotic in America but now, after 9/11, they are seen as signifying danger, along with other signifiers of the Muslim religion.

Cornflakes

Magnus Pyke
"The Influence of American Foods and Food Technology in Europe" in C. W. E. Bigsby, Ed. *Superculture : American Popular Culture and Europe*
Bowling Green, OH: Bowling Green University Popular Press (1975:85–86)

In certain respects, cornflakes and the diversity of other so-called "breakfast cereals" of the same category epitomize the basic characteristics of American foods, which themselves reflect

American style and philosophy. Ideas about right and wrong when extended to food, not only comprise views about the suitability or unsuitability of eating certain articles of diet, but are also concerned with eating behaviour which itself constitutes a major factor by which the social coherence of the community is maintained. Cornflakes and a whole series of similar products, including Nuttose, Grapenuts, Malta Vita, Cero-Frito and many more, were developed as part of the religious philosophy of the Seventh-Day Adventist community then settled in Battle Creek, Michigan. The original idea was that such food products were in some way peculiarly pure and therefore could be eaten straight out of the box and without further handling or preparation by those people most earnestly in search of spiritual purity. At the same time a great deal of attention was given to the mechanical details of the process by which these breakfast cereals were manufactured in order to produce a uniform, palatable and, consequently, commercially salable commodity. It followed that the social change which breakfast cereals can argued either to have brought about or, alternatively, assuming that the change was already happening, of which they were an indication, was only partly due to their purported religious significance and was perhaps to a much larger degree inherent in the technical ability, manufacturing skill and heavy expenditure on advertising taken by their devout—but business-like—American originators....

The style of twentieth century urban life, in which people increasingly believed in the inevitability of devoting the major proportion of their lives to industrial employment, called for exactly the qualities that cornflakes provided.

*   *   *

One of the comforting things about traveling around the world is that just about everywhere you go, you find breakfast cereals and, generally speaking, some version of Cornflakes. According to Magnus Pyke, the original reasons breakfast cereals were developed were connected to religious beliefs and a desire for purity. But this was soon eclipsed by their functionality, for packaged breakfast cereals relieved the housewife from having to cook hot cereal (this was before the microwave and instant hot cereals) and made it possible for men and women to eat a nutritional breakfast without anyone having to do any cooking. A good breakfast was important for people who were focusing their energies on work in the outside world. These foods were seen as what might be called "fuel foods," designed to fuel people who were on the go and hoping to find success in the business world.

Many of the packaged cereals that are now sold are full of sugar and are not healthy; they are contributing to the current obesity problem that starts as early as childhood. These cereals can be seen as a kind of candy in the form of cereal. Candy masquerades as cereal, which we used to assume—before we started reading the labels and found out what was in them—was good for those who ate them. Epidemiological studies show that toddlers who are overweight will probably stay overweight when they grow older and are at risk of becoming obese.

There are, on the other hand, many "healthy" cereals are gaining in popularity, which contain relatively little sugar and have high fiber content. Among the nutritious cereals, according to *Consumer Reports* and other sources, are All-Bran, Shredded Wheat ("an excellent source of Whole Grain" it says on the box), Grape-Nuts, and Fiber One (with fifty-seven percent of the daily fiber requirement and no sugar). Now that dieticians are stressing the importance of whole grains, Cheerios has become a whole-grain cereal.

As bad as many of the popular cereals are, at least youngsters ate them with milk and got some nutritional benefits from the milk. Now, studies suggest, many young people don't have cereal and milk or eat proper breakfasts but drink soda pop and eat sugary toaster pop-up snacks or so-called breakfast bars for breakfast. And some people, on diets or because they are too lazy to cook, eat packaged cereal for lunch or for dinner.

Post Shredded Wheat advises, on the back of the box, "Choose 2 meals a day and replace each with a serving of your favorite Post Healthy Classics, 1/2 cup of fat-free milk and 1/2 cup of fruit." This diet, what Post calls its "Eat 2 Lose 10 Plan" as part of a "reduced calorie diet" will supposedly help people lose ten pounds. Post also provides a website for those interested in following this diet. The connection of cereal to purity and to good health remains as one of the benefits of eating healthy cereals.

What Post doesn't say is that most people who lose weight gain it right back, regardless of their diet regimen. This suggests that those who lose weight on this diet are condemned, for eternity, to eating two meals of Post Shredded Wheat or one of their other "healthy" cereals if they wish to maintain their loss of weight or to be in a revolving door of losing weight, gaining it back, and losing weight again, endlessly. However it ends, Post and other healthy cereals, make out very well.

White Bread

Sigfried Giedion
Mechanization Takes Command: A Contribution to Anonymous History
W. W. Norton (1948:198–199)

Since mechanization, it has often been pointed out, white bread has become much richer in fats, milk, and sugar. But there are added largely to stimulate sales by heightening the loaf's eye-appeal. The shortenings used in bread, a leading authority states, are "primarily for the purpose of imparting desirable tender eating or chewing qualities to the finished product." They produce the "soft velvet crumb," a cakelike structure, so that the bread is half-masticated, as it were, before reaching the mouth.

About 6 percent of sugar is usually added to white bread. This too makes for looseness of structure and imparts a slight sweetness. Moreover it stimulates fermentation. But above all, sugar is "the source of crust color." If the amount is reduced, the thin crust becomes "pale and unattractive" in appearance instead of being infused with that golden-yellow gloss, like the bright red apples whose appetizing exterior has almost driven out other varieties of less dazzling appearance but more delicate flavor....

Long before mechanization set in, Sylvester Graham made it clear that the thin-crusted bread, made of finely milled flour, bakes more quickly than any other. Imperceptibly, public taste adapted itself to this fact. Today's arbiter of taste in the bread industry indicates to bakers what he considers the main defects in crust: toughness, thickness, cracks. And he recommends above all tenderness and uniformity.

* * *

Growing up in an "ethnic" family, I used to eat rye bread, pumpernickel bread, and other "Jewish" (read Polish and German, in origin) breads, bagels, and rolls. So I seldom ate packaged white breads like "Wonder Bread." I always marveled at the malleability of white bread, of the way you could press down on it and compact it and then it would spring back to its original form. What Giedion brings to the discussion of white bread is an analysis of the way that mechanization took control of the bread industry and of how the baking industry convinced people to change their taste preferences in favor of an easily manufactured quasi-cakelike bread with a "soft velvet crumb."

In his book, *The Structures of Everyday Life*, Fernand Braudel points out that in the 1780s peasants in France commonly ate two or three pounds of bread a day, because they had little else to eat. Bread was relatively inexpensive compared to other foods based on bread's caloric content. Braudel offers some statistics (figure 5.4) of interest about the relative cost of food for peasants.

Food	Times More Expensive than Bread
Meat	11
Fresh sea fish	65
Freshwater fish	9
Eggs	6

Figure 5.4   Relative Cost of Food for Peasants

We can see why bread played such an important part in the diet of ordinary people. In 1780, there was a National School of Bakery that was founded to improve the quality of white bread, which was replacing the other kinds of whole grain breads that were popular at the time. To this day, French artisan bread has been of exemplary quality, though for a time, French bakers seemed to have lost their way and French bread wasn't very good, as a rule.

In the United States, there has been a "bread" revolution in recent years and excellent artisan breads are now available in many large cities and other areas as well, generally in upscale supermarkets and bakeries. Some bakeries imported German bakers and brick ovens in which to make their breads. In San Francisco, sourdough bread is very popular, since the climate in San Francisco is optimal for making this kind of bread.

I've often wondered whether there was a correlation between the kind of spongy white bread that was popular in the United States and our political order. In the era of spongy white bread, there was less ideology and more of a spirit of compromise among our politicians. The development of crisp- crusted artisan breads, like those available in France, Germany, and Italy, has coincided with a growth in ideological ferment and, generally speaking, an unwillingness in many of our politicians in Washington, DC to compromise. Hard-crusted breads and hard liners in politics both seem to have come of age at the same time. And as our artisan breads gets crustier, our politicians become more ideological and less interested in making compromises.

Bagels

Stanley Regelson
"The Bagel: Symbol and Ritual at the Breakfast Table" in Arens,
The American Dimension: Cultural Myths and Social Realities
    Port Washington, NY: Alfred (1976:129–133)

The bagel (behgl), derived from the German *Baugel* (little bracelet) is a doughnut-shaped roll made from high-gluten flour. Simmered in boiling water for two minutes before baking, it has a unique chewy texture...The bagel itself is only one of a number of traditional Jewish small breads. Among the others are kaiser rolls, salt stengels, and bialystokers, which have faded into obscurity as the bagel has grown more popular. Because of their odd recipe, bagels are produced by specialized bakers in bagel factories, but never at home. Bagel factories, traditionally located in cellars, are numerous wherever there is a concentrated Jewish population. Jews living far from such centers now make provision for the shipment of frozen bagels, since the chemical additive that keeps bread fresh cannot be added to bagels without destroying the characteristic texture....

In recent years, the term "bagels-and-lox Judaism" has become a favorite theme of rabbinical sermons in the United States. It used to refer pejoratively to those Jews who avoid the synagogue and neglect traditional religious practices, yet adhere strongly to "frivolous" secular customs. Concretely, this translates into the fact that there are many Jews who will never voluntarily visit a synagogue, but manage to perform the bagel ritual every week.

... In Jewish culture, bread of any kind signifies man's material needs and is specifically seen as the symbol of earth itself. The prayer over bread refers to it as being brought forth from the earth, and also contains a reference to the first man, since the word for earth (*adamah*) contains Adam's name. Similar to a simplified folkview of the human body...the shape of the bagel symbolically represents a navel mediated between the earthly and the divine.

* * *

The rise of bagels as breakfast breads coincided with the development of an interest in crusty artisan breads in America. It may be that many Americans sampled good European bread while traveling abroad and developed a taste for it—along with a taste for espresso coffee and other foods. Over the years bagels have grown in size and the typical bagel now is very high in calories. One large bagel is equivalent to around five slices of bread as far as calories are concerned.

There are some packaged bagels that resemble "real" bagels in shape, but they don't have the real bagels textural density and taste. In part this is because these "imitation" bagels are not boiled before being baked, but also because the bakeries that make them don't use the same kind of wheat that traditional bagel makers use. Thus, these bagels are pseudobagels, impostors, pretending to be bagels and fooling large numbers of people who mistakenly think that anything in the shape of the bagel is a bagel.

In his article on bagels, Regelson goes into a long, convoluted description of how the typical combination of bagel, cream cheese, and lox (smoked salmon) has, symbolically speaking, a sexual dimension to it: the white cream cheese represents semen and the smoked salmon symbolizes menstrual blood and this combination has implications for religious beliefs Jews have about the coming of the Messiah and reflects the Jewish people's adherence to their Messianic faith. It is worth reading his analysis for those interested in how an artifact can be deconstructed on many different levels.

He also points out that many Jews have little connection with Judaism except in terms of things they eat. There are many "bagel-and-lox" Jews who have no affiliation with organized Judaism. We can modify Leon Poliakov's witty definition of French Jews as "people who instead of no longer going to church, no longer go to synagogues" and apply it to America. We can say about these "bagel-and-lox" Jews in America that they are people who don't go to synagogues (except, perhaps, for the high holy days), but keep their vague and tenuous identification with Judaism by eating bagels and lox. And not going to synagogues tactically speaking, is a mistake, because many of them serve bagels and lox, among other things, for their Oneg Shabbat lunches, held after Saturday services.

Myst

Janet H. Murray
Hamlet on the Holodeck: The Future of Narrative in Cyberspace
Cambridge, MA: MIT Press (1997:108–109, 140–141)

One of the limitations of the graphically immersive world of Myst is that it is dramatically static. Nothing happens of its own accord as the player wanders around in search of puzzles to solve. Myst sends us on a treasure hunt in a weirdly depopulated environment, a quest that is only partially motivated by the story. The lack of dynamic events reflects the simplicity of the underlying programming. *Myst* offers the interactor an elegant and seamless interface in which most of the activity of the game is moving forward through a space by mouse-clicking in the direction you wish to go. There are no enemies to encounter or people to bargain with. Few of the puzzles require any carrying of objects from one location to another. *Myst* is an unusually nonacquisitive and nonviolent game compared to most puzzle quests. The solution to the puzzles often depend on subtle aural cues, increasing the player's attentiveness to the meticulous sound design. In short, there is almost nothing to distract you in *Myst* from the densely textured visual and aural environment, but this intense immersion in visiting the place comes at the cost of a diminished immersion in an unfolding story....

Narrative satisfaction can be directly opposed to game satisfaction, as the endings of *Myst*, widely hailed as the most artistically successful story puzzle of the early 1990s make clear... The "winning" ending involves locating the good wizard Atrus and remembering to bring with you the magical item that will free him from captivity. This is a satisfyingly fair yet challenging Mystery plot.

Yet surprisingly, the "losing" endings of the game are much more satisfying than the winning ending... The most dramatically satisfying endings are the near-identical losing branches, which are the result of choosing to rescue either of the evil brothers.

*   *   *

Myst was created by Cyan, which sold about seven million copies of the game and made around $150 million on it. Cyan had a great deal of trouble finding a video-game publisher to distribute the game, but finally found one, Broderbund, that was willing to take a chance on publishing and distributing the game. It is an immersive game in which little happens, yet it has a powerful sound design that makes playing it a memorable experience. The sequel to *Myst* was *Riven*, which took five CDs to play. Cyan sold around a million-and-a-half copies of *Riven*. Both games are made of still images that rapidly change and give players the illusion of motion. From a programming perspective, they are relatively simple games, but they both have hypnotic power because they are so immersive and because the sound track is so beguiling.

In an article "(D)Riven" on *Riven* in *Wired*, Jon Carroll writes about Rand and Robyn Miller, who created both *Myst* and *Riven* (Issue 5.09, September 1977):

> Asked to define what they were doing, Rand used the phrase "immersive environments." None of them liked the word game anymore, because a game could be anything. Checkers is a game; *Riven* is an immersive environment. And the environment...had to be "familiar and strange." You had to feel that you had seen it before; you had to know that you had never seen it before."

In addition to being immersive, Janet H. Murray argues that video games provide agency—the power to take actions that are meaningful and have consequences in the game—and are transformative in that they allow shape shifting due to using morphing software.

Myst, we must remember, was released in 1993, so by video-game standards, it is very old. And since then there have been a number of important genres that have developed such as first-person shooter games, sports games, role-playing games, simulations. and teaching games. The video-game industry is enormous.

In 2004, $7.1 billion of software for video games was sold. It is estimated that the games and game-playing consoles and Internet versions of the games will reach around $31 billion in sales by 2010. Some games can be played on powerful computers that are designed specially for game playing, but most dedicated video-game players purchase video-game consoles, which now sell for between $300 and $600 and are really mini-supercomputers.

There are a number of biological, psychological, and social problems connected with playing video games. Players can suffer from repetitive stress injuries, can become obese due to a lack of exercise and snacking while playing, can fail to develop social skills necessary to get along with others, can become hyperactive when not playing video games, can become addicted to playing the games, and can become desensitized to violence, among other things. Some games are full of violence and sex, such as *Mortal Kombat V: Every Fatality, Grand Theft Auto: Vice City,* and *BMX XXX-Acclaim.*

There are also some benefits worth considering. Players often develop a sense of agency from playing video games and feel that they can have an impact on events. They also develop certain kinds of motor skills that may be of value and a kind of literacy that is functional in a technological age. Video games are also used to teach and to help people deal with their emotional problems, so there are positive aspects to video games as well as negative ones.

Furniture

Milton R. Sapirstein, M.D.
Paradoxes of Everyday Life
New York: Premier Books (1955:95–98)

As the car is the symbol of masculinity, so is the house a symbol of femininity. To a woman, her home is like another, larger body and all her mysterious impulses find expression within its walls. Her deepest self is implicated in the texture of the draperies, the casual shape of chairs and tables, the dimensions of a bed. As she trudges from shop to shop—examining, comparing, pondering over this article or that—her choices are determined by an unconscious image of what she is, or dreads to be....

The unconscious fear of "exposing" not their taste alone but their inmost selves is what drives a large number of women into the arms of professional decorators. By leaving decisions to the experts, they disengage themselves from the entire project. Or try to....

For instance...A girl with a strong unconscious masculine identification may adopt a starkly modernistic decor; its clean straight lines and lack of protuberances announce plainly the kind of body she would like to have had. But, if she is struggling against this tendency, she may feel the compulsion to "say it isn't so" and fill her home, as an acquaintance of mine did, with plump chairs and sofas in the Biedermaier style. This woman, incidentally, solved her conflict rather neatly. Her own study— where she pursued her scholarly researches and to which she rarely admitted anybody else—was in marked contrast to the rest of her house, severely functional, with not a curve in sight. It did not resemble her body, which was as stout and cushiony as the publicly-displayed furniture. But it did give visible form to the unconscious idea she had of herself, an idea further manifested in her lean and sinewy prose.

*   *   *

Buying furniture isn't simply a matter of economics and price comparisons but is connected, Sapirstein argues, with all kinds of unconscious phenomena that helps shape our decisions about what style of furniture to purchase and how to arrange it. These same unconscious imperatives are involved in our choices of clothes, but we can change our clothing styles easily, whereas our furniture says put for long periods of time—often for decades. Complicating this matter is the role of lifestyles in choosing furniture, for according to Mary Douglas, cultural alignment is the most important predictor of consumer choice. Families from different lifestyles might have the same amount of money available when choosing furniture but choose different styles of furniture. If Douglas is correct, the lifestyles of the families will ultimately shape their decisions about what kind of furniture to purchase rather than individual taste.

I once appeared on a radio show with Stanley Marcus of Neiman-Marcus. He informed me that one of the functions of his stores was to help oil-rich families fix up their homes in an acceptable style. These oil millionaires often were not educated and didn't know what kind of furniture and other accessories to purchase, so they relied on the salespeople at Neiman-Marcus, who had more elevated and sophisticated taste, to furnish their homes. I called this process "couthification."

Not only is the style of furniture important, but so too is the age of the furniture. Families with "old" money tend to furnish their homes with antiques and other furniture handed down over the years. Oak furniture was the rage for many years, and it still is with many people. Middle-class families often buy what we might call "Scandinavian modern" styles. In recent years, things have changed and now many middle-class families purchase "old" furniture in antique stores or other stores that sell this kind of furniture, so it is impossible to tell, in many cases, from a family's furniture, what class they come from. And a number of companies make furniture that looks old, to further complicate matters.

Teddy Bears

Jack Solomon
The Signs of Our Times: The Secret Meanings of Everyday Life
New York: Perennial Library (1990:88, 93)

A plethora of teddy bears in today's adult toy market is a sign of a disturbingly new emotional need prompted by the anxieties of the nuclear age. For teddy bears are not only surrogate children; they are also icons of a by-gone era. Along with a new generation of wooden rocking horses, the teddy bears of the 1980s recall a world that, at least from today's perspective, looks a great deal safer and more innocent than our own. Teddy bears first appeared around the turn of the century—they get their name from Teddy Roosevelt—and they still carry with them an aura of that relatively quiet epoch before the world wars.

We have become so beguiled by that aura that genuine survivors from the period have become not only collector's items but status symbols as well (an antique Steiff teddy bear was auctioned off for $8,237 in 1987). Belonging to the era of A.A. Milne rather than the post-Freudian world of Maurice Sendak, the teddy bear imaginatively takes us back to an ideal Edwardian utopia. Ideally ensconced within the nursery of a newly refurbished Victorian townhouse, surround by wooden rocking horses, cradles, and Laura Ashley wallpaper, teddy looks out on the timeless twilight of an era that has been forever lost but whose shadow can be captured by anyone who can afford the right props. He has survived both the nuclear and the space age, remaining as a talisman of genteel stability and tradition, a full-fledged, if modest, testimony to the mythic power of nostalgia....

Teddy bears recall for us the innocence of the world of Winnie-the-Pooh... "Hush, hush, whisper, who dares, Christopher Robin is saying his prayers." But he may be praying for a G.I. Joe Transportable Tactical Battle Platform. Well, why not? Toys are us.

*   *   *

We've only had Teddy Bears since the turn of the twentieth century and they are connected, Solomon suggests, to earlier times when people were more innocent. Psychoanalytically speaking, they help people regress to their childhoods, when they weren't subject to the stresses of conditional love and the later pressures of adulthood.

In *Mythologies*, Roland Barthes has a discussion of toys and argues that French toys reflect the fact that French adults see children as another self and that French toys always reflect important aspects of adult French life such as medicine, school, the army or air force, transportation, science, and the media. These toys present to children, he asserts, things that adults do not find as unusual, such as war, aliens, and bureaucracy. He mentions a little French doll that that urinates, has an esophagus, and wets its diapers. This doll prepares little girls for housekeeping and "conditions" her for her future role as a mother.

From a sociological perspective, toys have both manifest (obvious) and latent or covert (hidden) functions. The manifest function of toys is to entertain children, while the latent function of toys, as Barthes has suggested in *Mythologies*, is to prepare them for adult life. Toys also reflect a great deal about people's values and beliefs and their psychological and technological development. The teddy bear, Solomon reminds us, has given way to transformers and G.I. Joes and, since he wrote, to video games full of sexuality and violence. Teddy bears remind us, it would seem, of our lost innocence and our desire to have them reminds us that there are elements in our psyches that long for the security and peacefulness of the days when we actually were innocent.

Soap Powders and Detergents

Roland Barthes
Mythologies
New York: Hill & Wang (1957/1972:36–37)

These products have been in the last few years the object of such massive advertising that they now belong to a region of French daily life which the various types of psycho-analysis would do well to pay some attention to if they wish to keep up to date. One could then usefully contrast the psycho-analysis of purifying liquids (chlorinated, for example) with that of soap-powders (*Lux, Persil*) or that of detergents (*Omo*). The relations between the evil and the cure, between dirt and a given product, are very different in each case.

Chlorinated fluids, for instance, have always been experienced as a sort of liquid fire, the action of which must be carefully estimated, otherwise the object itself would be affected, "burnt" ... This type of product rests on the idea of a violent, abrasive modification of matter … the product "kills" the dirt. Powders, on the contrary, are separating agents: their ideal role is to liberate the object from its circumstantial imperfection: dirt is "forced out" and no longer killed. in the Omo imagery, dirt is a diminutive enemy, stunted and black, which takes to its heels from the fine immaculate linen at the sole threat of a judgment of *Omo* …

To say that *Omo* cleans in depth … is to assume that linen is deep, which no one had previously thought, and this unquestionably results in exalting it … As for foam, it is well-known that is signifies luxury … Foam can even be the sign of a certain spirituality, inasmuch as the spirit has the reputation of being able to make something out of nothing…. What matters is the art of having disguised the abrasive function of the detergent under the delicious image of a substance at once deep and airy which can govern the molecular order of the material without damaging it.

*   *   *

One of the interesting things about Roland Barthes' analysis of soap powders and detergents is how he classifies the different means of cleaning laundry: (1) soap powders, (2) detergents, and (3) purifying liquids. I have made a chart (figure 5.5) that shows how each of these kinds of cleaning agents represents, psychoanalytically speaking, something distinctive.

Foam, he suggests, represents luxury to people, and also has certain magical and spiritual implications—something

Purifying Liquids	Soap Powders	Detergents
Chlorinated	Separating agents *Lux, Persil*	Liberating agents *Omo*
Liquid fire		Cleans deep
Kills dirt	Keeps order	Foamy (luxury)

Figure 5.5   Soap Powders and Detergents and the Psyche

voluminous is made out of nothing to speak of. This is connected with a notion consumers have that matter is "airy." Foam also disguises the power of detergents, for detergents that foam only seem unsubstantial. In reality, they are powerful agents.

Barthes points out that an advertisement for *Omo* says it cleans in depth, which means then that "linen is deep." This, Barthes says, is an important revelation. Linen is obviously thin and flat physically speaking so it must be deep psychoanalytically speaking, which suggests, then, that when we purchase linens, there is more involved with our choice of linens than we might imagine and that unconscious pressures may be at play in our choices of bed sheets, pillows, and other linens. Finally, Barthes points out that while *Persil* and *Omo* are different in terms of the way they clean things, they are similar in one very important respect: they are both owned by the Anglo-Dutch company Unilever. Thus, international capitalism is found lurking in the shadows, behind the different brands in France, just as Procter & Gamble in the United States manufactures a number of different brands of detergents that are sold in many countries.

Vacuum Cleaners

Adrian Forty
Objects of Desire: Design & Society from Wedgwood to IBM
New York: Pantheon (1986:175–81)

The vacuum cleaner was first conceived in the United States. In 1860, a patent was taken out for a machine that both brushed and sucked up dust, and with the next few years a number of similar devices were patented, although none was put into commercial production. It was not until the 1890s that the first vacuum cleaners were put on the market. By this time there was good reason for wanting a device to replace the duster and broom: the fear of germ-laden dust had begun to settle in people's minds, reinforce by strong propaganda against the evils of dry dusting ...

In selling vacuum cleaners, manufacturers were quick to emphasize their hygienic properties. The arguments for vacuum cleaners as labour-saving devices were not particularly convincing: Christine Frederick, an American household efficiency expert, had shown in 1920 that vacuum cleaners saved little time though they did the job more efficiently. Consequently, it was as instruments of hygiene that vacuum cleaners were generally advertised. The advice that Christine Frederick (who had become a marketing consultant to domestic appliance companies) gave to the British electrical goods industry in 1927 on how to sell vacuum cleaners was to stress their hygienic qualities and to use the familiar anxiety-inducing arguments to drive the message home. Having explained the faults of old-fashioned cleaning methods, she continued:

The principle behind all new cleaning methods is not scattering but *absorption of dust.* This new principle is exemplified in the many dustless and specially treated dustcloths and mops, but reaches the height of perfection in the electric suction cleaner... There had been little technical development in domestic electric vacuum cleaners since their introduction in 1910, but the visual change in them was so great that the early designs now seem quaint and archaic.

*   *   *

Objects and artifacts are frequently based upon desires and long-standing needs that people have, which means that it is possible to trace the development of various objects as they evolve over the years. We can do this with vacuum cleaners, which were large and relatively primitive devices in their earliest manifestations. It has been more than one hundred years since they were invented, and during this period of time they have evolved a great deal, even if the basic principle of the device has not.

They have also taken on other functions, and now many vacuum cleaners can also be used to wash and clean rugs as well as to suck up dust and other small objects that may have fallen on them. In addition, many vacuum cleaners now don't have bags but have containers that can be emptied, saving users from the bother of having to install bags after they've thrown out filled bags. These filled bags remind us how much dust, hair, and other kinds of dirt was in our homes, and, to the extent we find dirt psychologically disturbing, getting rid of them means that vacuum cleaners are less intimidating now. We have to empty the container but that doesn't have the psychologically repugnant resonance that a bag full of dirt and dust has.

In recent years, there has been a technological breakthrough in the design of vacuum cleaners that has energized the industry. A British designer developed a vacuum cleaner that has separate compartments for power and for the stuff the cleaner picked up, so the power of the vacuum is not diminished as the bag fills with debris. This innovation is now available on small hand vacuums as well. For those who love the newest technologies, there is now a small self-guided robot vacuum cleaner that wanders around rooms, cleaning stuff up without anyone guiding it. The next step, I would imagine, would be to teach vacuum cleaners how to empty themselves.

Computers

Susan B. Barnes
Computer-Mediated Communication: Human-to-Human Communication Across the Internet
Boston: Allyn & Bacon (2003:12, 18)

CMC creates media environments by enabling people to communicate with each other. When talking about CMC, a distinction needs to be made between using computers as a technology and using them as a tool. When people use computers to perform tasks such as word processing or database retrieval, they are using them as tools. In contrast, when people are communicating with other people through a computer network, they are using the computer as a medium of communication...When people engage in CMC [computer-mediated communication], they use computers to connect to a network of other people to exchange information and ideas. This new intellectual and social environment is often called cyberspace...Once an isolating productivity tool, networked computers now support the acquisition, creation, and exchange of communication between individuals, groups, and organizations....

During the 1950s, computers were introduced into business settings. Studies of office automation began to appear in the early 1960s...Pioneering CMC researchers argued that the elimination of visual and verbal information and direct feedback from interpersonal correspondence would make computers a "cold" medium in which people would not build emotional attachments. They believed that the plain-text characteristic of e-mail would make it difficult for people to understand situations and communicate with each other. This became known as the **cues-filtered-out** perspective...In contrast to this early research, Rice and Love...discovered a percentage of CMC contains **socioemotional content**. Rice and Love define socioemotional content "as interactions that show solidarity, tension relief, agreement, antagonism, tension and disagreement." People use CMC to share interpersonal information....

Although CMC correspondents are physically separated, interpersonal relationships do develop through the Internet. In some instances, levels of affection and emotion that develop through CMC relationships can equal or surpass face-to-face relationships.

*   *   *

In recent years we've recognized that computers are devices, whatever else they may be and whatever else they can do, that facilitate communication between people. Young people nowadays, who have grown up with computers, cannot appreciate how revolutionary computers are and what an impact they have made in our everyday lives. Let me offer an example.

Before the development of the Internet and email, if professors wanted to send a book manuscript to an editor, they had to type it out (and sometimes type several drafts of it, which took a great deal of time) and then mail their revised draft to their editor. Now, with the computer and the development of word processing, professors can revise their books as many times as they wish without having to retype the whole manuscript, and then email a file of the book, in an instant, to their editors.

Editors email manuscripts to copy editors, who check them over for typing mistakes and other errors. Before we had computers, copy editors for the book would write on the margins or use sticky notes to ask questions to the author about proposed revisions to the manuscript and mail the manuscript back to the author. Now, most copy editors make their changes on the file of the book sent to them by the author. They then send the file of the manuscript with their suggestions back to the author for confirmation that the proposed changes should be made.

People who wish to travel can now book hotel rooms all over the world and communicate with hotels, restaurants, travel agents, and others involved in the tourism industry by using the Internet. With the computer phone company, Skype, phone calls within the United States to other Skype users are free and calls to foreign countries only cost pennies. Using Skype and other similar programs, webcams enable people to talk to and see one another over the Internet at no cost.

The notion that email cannot express emotion seems, to me, patently absurd. It's like saying that printed works, such as novels, short stories, and poems can't express emotion. It isn't one's facial expression that is important; it is what one writes that is crucial. But even if you don't deal with what is written in emails (i.e., with the content of the message), the fact is that writers using email can use different type sizes, different colors, and now emoticons, which explicitly reflect emotions.

☺   ☹

Some emoticons are in the form of images and not just made up of keystrokes from the keyboard. And there are dozens of different emoticons that writers can use.

Barnes' distinction between computers used as tools (such as for word processing and Powerpoint presentations) and as communication devices makes good sense. For large numbers of people it is the computer's use as a communication device that is most useful and important for them. The Internet has changed everything in the media world and the Internet is, in essence, a facilitator of communication of all kinds.

The impact of the computer has been truly revolutionary. Nowadays, young children with video-game players have more computing power at their disposal than engineering professors or generals had just a decade or two ago. A number of scholars are now raising ethical questions about how we should deal with computers and with so-called technological imperatives. This is because computers have the power to reshape our societies and cultures and some of the directions that computers are leading us may not be good for us—as individuals and as members of societies. How to respond to the ethical challenges posed by computers is a major problem occupying philosophers and politicians.

CHAPTER 6

Learning Games and Activities

What follows are some learning games and activities that will help you apply theories and concepts that you have learned in the book in entertaining ways. I suggest that the games be played in groups of three sitting in a triangular formation with one person having good handwriting designated as the "scribe." The scribe participates in the discussions but also writes down the answers to each game based on a consensus among the players.

In some games there are really no "correct" answers. What is interesting is to find out whether there are areas of agreement about various matters, such as what you would spend $2,500 on if you had it to use on a spending spree or what the personality of car buyers is that makes them purchase a Saab rather than a BMW, if both cost about the same. When you work in teams, please find ways to agree on your team answers to the questions posed.

Time Capsule

Time capsules are containers filled with representative objects, buried and not dug up until fifty or a hundred years (or more) have passed. In this game, you list in order of importance the

1.	2.	3.
4.	5.	6.
7.	8.	9.
10.	11.	12.

Figure 6.1 Time Capsule Learning Exercise

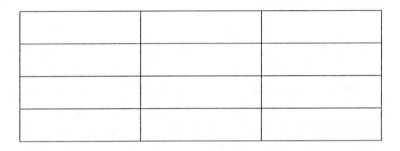

Figure 6.2 Visit America Brochure Exercise

twelve most important objects (and their brands, when possible) that best reflect American culture as of 2010 or whatever year it is when you are playing this game (figure 6.1). What will be interesting to see is how much agreement there will be—assuming there will be some agreement—among the different groups about which objects/artifacts are most representative of American culture and society.

Visit America Brochure

You are the art directors of an advertising agency. A company that sells tours of America comes to you and asks you to prepare a brochure to send to people in foreign countries who are interested in visiting the United States. Imagine twelve images to put into a brochure to give foreigners an idea of the most important sites for tourists in the United States. Write a brief description of each image in the boxes in figure 6.2.

Your Brands and What They Reveal

In the figure 6.3, list twelve things you own, and their brands, in order of their importance to you. Do not sign this form, but leave an identifier (a number of a word you've made up) so you can get it back after the exercise has concluded. The charts will

1.	2.	3.
4.	5.	6.
7.	8.	9
10.	11.	12.

Identifier:

Figure 6.3 Brands Exercise

Object	UU	LU	UM	LM	UL	LL
Automobile						
MP3 player						
Cell phone						
TV set						
Soda pop						
Hamburger						
Sunglasses						
Wristwatches						

Figure 6.4 Socioeconomic Classes and Brands

be circulated and your classmates will be asked to make guesses about what kind of a person made the list, based on the possessions and their brands. It will be interesting to see whether there are many similarities in terms of the objects and brands owned by the members of your class.

Socioeconomic Classes and Brands

In this exercise, we try to determine which brands would be used by members of the six socioeconomic classes that a sociologist, W. Lloyd Warner, said exist in the United States. They are: Upper-Upper, Lower-Upper, Upper-Middle, Lower-Middle, Upper-Lower, and Lower-Lower. Warner suggested that the common man and woman were members of either the Lower-Middle or Upper-Lower class. There are no "right" answers to this exercise. What will be interesting to see is whether we can determine things about people we see or know by placing objects by their socioeconomic class (figure 6.4).

Audi A5 $26,900	Lexus ES350 $32,000	BMW 328i $33,600	Mercedes E320 $33,000
Saab 9–3 $30,000	Volvo S40 $28,000	Kia Optima $17,000	Hummer H2 $60,000
Porsche 911 $76,000	Honda Fit $14,700	Jaguar XF $49,000	Mini-Cooper $18,500

Figure 6.5 Automobiles and Personality Types

Automobiles and Personality

A person might have around $35,000 to spend on a new car. Why does he or she purchase an Audi, Lexus, BMW, Mercedes, or Saab? If we assume that each brand of automobile appeals to a certain kind of person, the question is—what kind of person likes a Saab or Mercedes or any other automobile in a certain price range. Describe their personalities. I've given prices taken from *Consumer Reports* (figure 6.5).

Spending Spree

As a result of passing in the best term paper on semiotics and consumer culture, you win $2,500, but the money must be spent

Purchase	Cost	Brand

Figure 6.6 Shopping Spree

Insights and Interesting Things Learned in This Book

1.	2.	3.
4.	5.	6.
7.	8.	9.
10.	11.	12.

Figure 6.7   Insights and Interesting Ideas Found in Book

on a shopping spree. In figure 6.6, list what you would purchase and the approximate cost. The aim of this exercise is to compare the lists of purchases to see if there are any agreements among your classmates on what people would spend their money on.

Insights and Interesting Ideas

I describe an insight as the recognition of a relationship between or among things that you never realized existed before. An insight also involves learning something about the way a theory or concept can be applied to some aspect of life that reveals new things to you. In figure 6.7, list some of the insights you have gained from this book. If you can't think of insights, list some of most interesting things you learned from reading this book.

CHAPTER 7

Coda

Most of us spend a great deal of time shopping, and except for groceries and other consumables, we tend to keep what we buy. So we end up accumulating a lot of "stuff," even if we give a lot of it away to Goodwill or other charities. It's only when we move and start packing up what we have in our houses and apartments into cardboard boxes that we recognize how much we have. But our "collecting" mentality may be changing. As a result of the economic recession of 2008 and 2009 Americans have scaled back the amount of goods they purchase and have actually begun saving money, now that they cannot use their homes as ATM machines anymore. As President Barack Obama explained recently, the days of "voracious" overconsumption in the United States are over.

The Origins of the Objects of Our Affection

Once we decide what to buy (and our decision making on this matter is a subject of consuming interest to manufacturers and market researchers), we generally don't think very much about our purchases—except, perhaps, how to pay for them. In the United States, we know that much of what we buy was made in Asia but we don't know much about the origins of the things we use. That's why Ralph Linton's classic essay, "One Hundred Percent American," is such a revelation. A short selection from his discussion of the "American" bathroom follows:

> On awakening, he glances at the clock, a medieval European invention, uses one potent Latin word in abbreviated form, rises in haste, and goes to the bathroom...The insidious foreign influence pursues him even here. Glass was invented by the ancient Egyptians, the use of glazed tiles for floors and walls in the Near East, porcelain in China and the art of enameling on metal by Mediterranean artisans of the Bronze Age. Even his bathtub and toilet are but slightly modified copies of Roman originals....As he scans the latest editorial pointing out the dire results to our institutions of accepting foreign ideas, he will not fail to thank a Hebrew God in an Indo-European language that he is a one hundred percent (decimal system invented by the Greeks) American (from Americus Vespucci, Italian geographer).

Linton wrote this essay in 1937 for *The American Mercury*. I can only imagine what he would have added to it were he writing the piece today.

We live in an era when commerce is global, when people purchase objects made in many different lands in various "international" stores, and eat foods and drink beverages that are popular in many countries. Coffee, Linton points out, is an Abyssinian plant discovered by Arabs, sugar was discovered in India, and cream comes from Asia Minor. In our postmodern societies, as I explained in my discussion of the ideas of Lyotard, we consciously revel in an eclectic approach to culture. Things have changed, Lyotard argues, and no longer do we want to be one hundred percent American or French or anything. Instead, we want to have the best from everywhere and live international-style lives.

The Complexity of Objects

Objects, artifacts, things, "stuff," whatever we want to call the examples of material culture I've dealt with, are very complex and can reveal a great deal to us, if we know what questions to ask of them. For one thing, manufactured objects reflect a certain level of technological expertise. So objects tell us something about how advanced the society was that produced the manufactured artifact.

They also reflect the aesthetic sensibilities of the age in which they were made, as filtered through the consciousness of the designer of the artifact. Every artifact reflects certain notions of what is tasteful, attractive, or functional, so our objects tell us a good deal about aesthetics. They tell us something about both the designers and the purchasers of objects. If there are competing lifestyles, as Mary Douglas asserts, these lifestyles must have competing aesthetic sensibilities that enable members of a given lifestyle to determine what is proper and what isn't proper for them.

Consider blue jeans, for example. There are now many different kinds of blue jeans that are available and brands which compete with one another. There are tight-fitting ones, loose fitting ones, lined ones, acid-washed ones, faded ones, torn ones, deep Indigo ones, low waist ones and now, high waist ones, and so on. This means consumers desiring to buy a pair of blue jeans now have to consider any number of different brands and stylistic possibilities within each brand, leading in some cases to what might be described as the "agony of choice."

It is possible for those with an historical bent of mind to trace the evolution of objects from the time when they are first created to their most contemporary manifestations. You can see how toasters, vacuum cleaners, coffee makers and all kinds of other objects have evolved over time and each stage in their evolution tells us something about the technological prowess and canons of taste at the time when they were made or became popular. In contemporary America there is a vogue for "retro" toasters and a number of other retro objects, which take us back to earlier times. These "retro" objects then have a meaning and reflect something about our collective psyches.

Another matter to consider is how objects are advertised. We can get a good deal of insight into the cultural significance of products by looking at the advertisements and commercials that are made to sell them. Thus, Roland Barthes pointed out that if detergents clean deep, it must mean that sheets are deep, psychologically speaking, that is. Objects and artifacts of all kinds don't exist in a vacuum. They are based on calculations about who will use them, notions about public taste and many other considerations. Marshall McLuhan's book *The Mechanical Bride* uses advertisements for objects, among other things, to deal with what these object reflect about American culture and society. Roland Barthes also is concerned with many aspects of French material culture in his book *Mythologies* and with Japanese material culture in *Empire of Signs*.

People Watching and Artifact Analysis

What we call "people watching" involves, among other things, analyzing the clothes a given person is wearing, and the other objects they display, in an effort to gain a sense of what that person is like. We observe the cut and fabric and style of their clothing. We also scrutinize such things as their eyeglasses, the designs on men's ties, women's handbags and other style accessories such as their rings and other jewelry and their shoes. We look at all of these things and try to figure out what they reveal about the socioeconomic class of the people we are watching. We also look at people's faces to see whether we can "read" their facial expressions, though we all know that people often "lie" with their facial expressions. That's what acting is all about. Reading people is complicated because, for a variety of reasons, people often dress "down" or dress "up," which makes it difficult for us to determine what they are like, what social class they come from, and similar matters.

Just as we can use artifacts to watch people, we can use artifacts to "watch" a culture and if we are careful, we can often gain valuable insights into the cultures and societies where these artifacts are found. We must keep in mind, however, that analyzing objects is always a risky business, because it is sometimes impossible to determine what objects *really* reflect about individuals who use them or the cultures and societies where they are found. All that we can do, generally speaking, is make a case that a reasonable person would find worth considering and leave it there—for interpretations of all kinds are always subject to dispute.

We cannot compute the "meanings" of our things on a slide-rule and yet we all have an innate curiosity about material culture and what it can tell us. But if we can't be certain about what objects "mean," we can, at least, entertain interesting hypotheses about them, and if these hypotheses are congruent with findings by other kinds of social scientist and researchers, all the better. The objects we buy, we must remember, are objects of our affection and explaining affection, or, in some cases, passion (as in the case of some collectors), or even love, remains an enigma for all involved.

In this book I have suggested that the products we purchase have major importance for their sign values and this may be more important, in many cases, than the functions of the products. Thus, if one wants to listen to music with an MP3 player, there are many different brands of these devices from we can choose. The iPod is the dominant brand of MP3 player, in part because of its elegant styling and its superb functionality, but it is also more expensive than many other brands of these devices.

The MP3 Shuffle and the Pastiche

The iPod shuffle, which has no buttons on it, has been panned by many technology critics. Apple placed the controls for this device on the ear bud wires, and this angered many people who wished to be able to use their own ear buds or earphones. The shuffle is, I would suggest, a symbol of the postmodern sensibility. The shuffle is to sound what the pastiche is to images. When you listen to an MP3 using the shuffle for playing music on your player, you hear short selections from the various CDs that you've put on your computer. This contrasts with hearing entire albums. On my MP3 players, I have selections from Sondheim's *Company,* Beethoven string quartets, opera arias by Maria Callas, songs sung by Marlene Dietrich, Jacques Brel, Carlos Gardel, piano music played by Oscar Peterson, Mozart piano concertos, and so on.

The pastiche involves the playful mixing of styles and genres and selections from a variety of sources. The term is generally used for works of art that mix all kinds of things together: drawings, paintings, photographs, bits and pieces of newspapers, and that kind of thing. The pastiche is important because critics suggest it reflects the postmodern sensibility, being made of many different things. It tends to be playful, ironic, and self-referential.

Thus, when people listen to their CDs on an iPod shuffle or on other MP3 players on shuffle, they are involved with the auditory version of the pastiche. I have three MP3 players and I have them all on shuffle, though I could have them play entire albums, because I find the mixture of music stimulating and pleasant. You never know what will come next. I listen to albums of music on my stereo player.

The pastiche, an art form made of a variety of images, can be seen as a reflection of the breakdown of metanarratives found in postmodern societies. The pastiche is made of bits and pieces and is not a "coherent" art form, like a portrait or a landscape. With the shuffle, we have broken up the integrity and coherence of works of music such as string quartets, symphonies, albums by singers, musical comedies and so on and put them all together, serially, in fragments. This reflects what might be called an attack on style or an example of the development of a sense of stylelessness that is found in the way that people keep reinventing themselves and changing their identities.

Mike Featherstone discusses this matter of stylelessness and its relationship to the pastiche in his book *Consumer Culture & Postmodernism.* He writes (1991:26):

> There is less interest in constructing a coherent style than in playing with and expanding the range of familiar styles. The term style suggests coherence and hierarchical ordering of elements, some inner form and expressiveness...

He adds that attitudes about lifestyles are also changing and there are now no dominant lifestyles; rather, individuals are more or less creating their own lifestyles and changing them when they get bored with them.

The Semiotic Perspective and Being "Far Out"

This book has been informed by an applied semiotic perspective, in conjunction with psychoanalytic, sociological and ideological theories. Saussure pointed out that the science of signs dealt with signs in society, so there is an implicitly sociological and cultural dimension to my semiotic analysis of cultural and symbolic behavior. Peirce suggested that everything in the universe is "perfused with" or made entirely of signs, which means there's an enormous amount of things to analyze for semioticians.

Semiotics is an interpretive discipline; the name of the game is to use semiotic theory to make sense of things, to apply the theory to whatever topic is of interest. In this book, I have used semiotics, along with other disciplines, to deal with various aspects of consumer culture and, in particular, its role in shaping our identities as we "brand" ourselves.

Brands and the Self

I have devoted a chapter in this book to the importance of brands. Many people use brands of objects such as hats, suits, blue jeans, eyeglasses, sunglasses, handbags, messenger bags, attaché cases, and shoes to project an image of themselves, to help establish their identities. When it comes to consumer cultures, everything we purchase not only is a sign but has a brand. Some of these brands are internationally known and have meanings to everyone while other brands, such as store brands for foods and other products found in supermarkets and other kinds of stores, are not advertised at all. I cannot think of a single article of clothes or object that I've purchased that did not have a brand. One may purchase a "generic" hot dog from a hot dog stand, but in many cases the brand of hot dogs is written on the cart. When we buy food at a restaurant, the name of the restaurant is a "brand," whether it is a single restaurant or one of a chain of restaurants.

In the Middle Ages, Johan Huizinga tells us in his book *The Waning of the Middle Ages,* even bells had names. He mentions two bells, "big Jacqueline" and "Roland" in his book. Our cats and dogs all have names and their breeds also have names. Even mixed breeds, such as cockapoos, have names. We also name horses, cows, and other animals. We might even assert that our personal names are a kind of brand, except that there are often many others with our same names. I know of two other Arthur Bergers, though their middle names are different from mine. I started using my middle name, Asa, because people confused my work with that of another Arthur Berger, who taught at Brandeis University.

There are large numbers of John Smiths and Jane Browns and other common names in America. Our names often tell others something about our parents and about us, such as our religion, race, gender (though some names are unisexual), and perhaps our socioeconomic class. Brands can be looked upon as a form of naming things and using that name to confer certain notions about the value of things. In some cases, such as in fashion, the name of the designer is the brand. Georgio Armani is both a name and a brand.

Semiotics: It's Still With Me

I would describe myself as "mechant," a French term that means, roughly speaking, being mischievous. I like to play around with ideas and sometimes follow them to strange conclusions. My students used to describe me as a "far-out" thinker. I explained to them that just the opposite was the case. I was in the center and they were "far in," by which I meant that many concepts that are widely accepted by social scientists struck them as absurd or ridiculous. It was psychoanalytic theory, in particular, that generated their incredulity.

In part that was because they had never been exposed to Freudian psychoanalytic theory, and when they first heard me lecture on this topic and apply it to various topics, they were shocked. That is the way many of us deal with new and unfamiliar ideas. For example, my hypothesis that women's handbags have a sexual dimension and can be seen as reflections of the way they think about their sexual apparatus might strike someone as far-fetched. I would suggest that it is a hypothesis worth entertaining.

I find it amusing that some critics have suggested that my writings essentially involve synthesizing theories and ideas from others, which means that my work is essentially descriptive, explaining to others what is already known. So for my students I was far out or for my critics all I did was write about what is obvious, what everyone knows. The nice thing about postmodernism is that it allows both descriptions, which contradict one another, to be considered and perhaps be true at the same time.

I would hope that this book will help you, my readers, better understand the role semiotics can play in interpreting consumer culture and everyday life, and some insights about material culture and its role in our everyday lives. I define an insight as discovering that a relationship exists between things and ideas of which you were previously unaware. I believe that learning some of the basic concepts of semiotics will give you a methodology that you can apply not only to consumer culture but to your life, in general.

I happened to bump into a former student of mine in a supermarket recently. She studied with me in many years ago, in 1983. "That semiotics you taught us," she said. "It's still with me. And I find it useful all the time." I would hope that the theories and applications of semiotics you've learned in this book will be with you for long after you've read this book.

Bibliography

Adamy, Janet. (2006) "For Subway, Every Nook and Cranny on the Planet Is Possible Site for a Franchise," *The Wall Street Journal*. Sept. 11, Page A11.

Alsop, R. (2008) "The 'Trophy Kids' Grow Up: How the Millenial Generation Is Shaking Up the Workplace," *The Wall Street Journal*. Oct. 21.

Arens, W. and Susan P. Montague (eds.). (1976) *The American Dimension: Cultural Myths and Social Realities*. Port Washington, NY: Alfred.

*Bakhtin, Mikhail. M. (ed. Michael Holquist). Transl. Caryl Emerson and Michael Holquist. (1981) *The Dialogic Imagination: Four Essays*. Austin: University of Texas Press.

*———. Transl. Hélène Iswolsky. (1984) *Rabelais and His World*. Bloomington: Indiana University Press.

Barthes, Roland. Transl. Annette Lavers. (1972) *Mythologies*. New York: Hill & Wang.

———. Transl. Richard Howard. (1982) *Empire of Signs*. New York: Hill & Wang.

Barnes, Susan B. (2002) *Computer-Mediated Communication: Human-to-Human Communication Across the Internet*. Boston: Allyn & Bacon.

Baudrillard, Jean. Transl. James Benedict. (1968/1996) *The System of Objects*. London: Verso.

Baudrillard, Jean. Transl. C.T. (1970/1998). *The Consumer Society: Myths and Structures*. London: Sage.

Berger, Arthur Asa. (1984) *Signs in Contemporary Culture: An Introduction to Semiotics*. New York: Longman.

———. (1989) *Agitpop: Political Culture and Communication Theory*. New Brunswick, NJ: Transaction.

———. (ed.) (1989) *Political Culture and Public Opinion*. New Brunswick, NJ: Transaction.

Berger, Arthur Asa. (1995) *Cultural Criticism: A Primer of Key Concepts.* Thousand Oaks, CA: Sage.

———. (1997) *Bloom's Morning: Coffee, Comforters, and the Secret Meaning of Everyday Life.* Boulder, CO: Westview.

———. (2003) *Ads, Fads and Consumer Culture (Second Edition).* Boulder, CO: Rowman & Littlefield.

———. (2003) *Durkheim Is Dead: Sherlock Holmes Is Introduced to Sociological Theory.* Walnut Creek, CA: AltaMira.

Berger, John. (1972) *Ways of Seeing.* New York: Penguin.

Bigsby, Christopher W.E. (ed.) (1975) *SuperCulture: American Popular Culture and Europe.* Bowling Green, OH: Bowling Green Popular Press.

Blonsky, Marshall. (1992) *American Mythologies.* New York: Oxford University Press

Brasch, R. (1961) *How Did It Begin?* New York: Pocket Books.

Braudel, Fernand. Transl. Sian Reynolds. (1981) *The Structures of Everyday Life: The Limits of the Possible.* New York: Harper & Row.

Brenner, Charles. (1974) *An Elementary Textbook of Psychoanalysis (Revised Edition).* Garden City, NY: Anchor.

Briggs, Asa. (1988) *Victorian Things.* London: B.T. Batsford.

Burros, Marian. (2006) "Eating Well Notebook," *The New York Times.* Sept. 13, Page D5.

Carroll, Jon. (1977) "(D)Riven," *Wired.* Sept. Issue 5.09 http://www.wired.com/wired/5.09/riven.html.

Chandler, Daniel. (2002) *Semiotics: The Basics.* London: Routledge.

Chase, Marilyn. (1982) "Your Suit Is Pressed, Hair Neat, But What Do Your Molars Say?" *The Wall Street Journal.* June 16.

Coward, Rosalind and John Ellis. (1977) *Language and Materialism: Developments in Semiology and the Theory of the Subject.* London: Routledge & Kegan Paul.

Brooker, Peter. (1999) *Cultural Theory: A Glossary.* London: Arnold.

Certeau, Michel de. Transl. Steven Rendall. (1984) *The Practice of Everyday Life.* Berkeley: University of California Press.

Culler, Jonathan. (1986) *Ferdinand de Saussure (Revised Edition).* Ithaca, NY: Cornell University Press.

Danesi, Marcel. (2002) *Understanding Media Semiotics.* London: Arnold.

DeNitto, Denis. (1985) *Film, Form & Feeling.* New York: Harper & Row.

Dichter, Ernest. (2002) *The Strategy of Desire.* New Brunswick, NJ: Transaction.

Dokoupil, Tony. (2008) "Political Ties: How the Presidential Candidates Knot Their Neckties and What It Says About Them." *Newsweek.* Oct. 14, 2008.

Douglas, Mary. (1997) "In Defence of Shopping" in Pasi Falk and Colin Campbell (eds.) *The Shopping Experience.* London: Sage.

Durham, Meenakshi. G. and Douglas Kellner (eds.). (2001) *Media and Cultural Studies: Keyworks.* Malden, MA: Blackwell.

Eco, Umberto. (1976) *A Theory of Semiotics.* Bloomington: Indiana University Press.

Embler, Weller. (1966) *Metaphor and Meaning.* DeLand, FL: Everett/ Edwards.

Erikson, Erik H. (1963) *Childhood and Society (Second Edition).* New York: W.W. Norton.

Esslin, Martin. (1982) *The Age of Television.* San Francisco: W.H. Freeman.

Ewen, Stuart. (1976) *Captains of Consciousness: Advertising and the Social Roots of the Consumer Culture.* New York: McGraw-Hill.

Fairclough, Gordon and Janet Adamy (2000). "For Subway, Every Nook and Cranny on the Planet Is Possible Site for Franchise," *The Wall Street Journal.* Sept. 11, Page A11.

Falk, Pasi and Colin Campbell (eds.). (1997) *The Shopping Experience.* London: Sage.

Featherstone, Mike. (1991) *Consumer Culture & Postmodernism.* London: Sage.

Forty, Adrian. (1986) *Objects of Desire: Design & Society from Wedgwood to IBM.* New York: Pantheon.

Freud, Sigmund. Transl. Joan Riviere. (1962) *A General Introduction to Psychoanalysis (Revised Edition).* New York: Washington Square Press.

Fromm, Erich. (1962) *Beyond the Chains of Illusion: My Encounters with Marx and Freud.* New York: Simon & Schuster.

Garber, Marjorie. (1992) *Vested Interests: Cross-Dressing and Cultural Anxiety.* New York: Harper.

Geertz, Clifford. (1973) *The Interpretation of Cultures.* New York: Basic Books.

Giedion, Sigfried. (1969) *Mechanization Takes Command: A Contribution to Anonymous History.* New York: W.W. Norton.

Goffman, Erving. (1959) *The Presentation of Self in Everyday Life.* Garden City, NY: Doubleday.

Gorney, Rockerick. (1972) *The Human Agenda.* Reviewed in *Newsweek,* June 12, Page 100.

Hall, Stuart (ed.). (1997) *Representation: Cultural Representations and Signifying Practices.* London: Sage.

Hawkes, Terrence. (1977) *Structuralism and Semiotics.* Berkeley: University of California Press.

Hinsie, Leland E. and Robert. J. Campbell. (1970) *Psychiatric Dictionary.* New York: Oxford University Press

Jameson, Fredric. (1991) *Postmodernism or, The Cultural Logic of Late Capitalism.* Durham, NC: Duke University Press.

Jenks, Chris. (ed.) (1998). Core Sociological Dichotomies. London: Sage.

Johnson, Anna. (2002) *Handbags: The Power of the Purse.* New York: Workman.

Johnson, Lois Joy (2008). "The New Hair Color Rules," *More.* July/Aug., Page 68.

Klapp, Orrin. (1962) *Collective Search for Identity.* New York: Holt, Rinehart and Winston.

Klein, Melanie and Joan Riviere. (1937/1964) *Love, Hate and Reparation.* New York: W.W. Norton.

Kotler, Philip, John Bowen, and James Makens. (1999) *Marketing for Hospitality and Tourism (Second Edition).* Upper Saddle River, NJ: Prentice-Hall.

Lakoff, George and Mark Johnson. (1980) *Metaphors We Live By.* Chicago: University of Chicago Press.

Lefebvre, Henri. Transl. Sacha Rabinovich. (1971) *Everyday Life in the Modern World.* New York: Harper Torchbooks.

Linton, Ralph. (1937). "One Hundred Percent American." *The American Mercury,* 40: 1937, Pages 427–429.

Lifton, Robert Jay. (1970). *History and Human Survival.* New York: Random House.

Linn, Allison (2006). "Smaller Houses Thrive in Starbuck's Shadow," *The San Francisco Examiner.* Sept. 11.

Lotman, Yuri. Transl. Mark E. Suino. (1976) *Semiotics of Cinema.* Ann Arbor: Michigan Slavic Contributions.

———. Transl. Gail Lenhoff and Ronald Vroom. (1977) *The Structure of the Artistic Text.* Ann Arbor: Michigan Slavic Contributions.

Lury, Celia. (2004). *Brands: The Logos of the Global Economy.* London: Routledge.

Lyotard, Jean-François. Transl. Geoff Bennington and Brian Massumi. (1984) *The Postmodern Condition: A Report on Knowledge.* Minneapolis: University of Minnesota Press.

MacFarquhar, Neil. (2006) "A Simple Scarf But Meaning Much More Than Faith," *The New York Times.* Sept. 8, Page A20.

Marx, Karl. (1964) Transl. T.B. Bottomore. *Preface to the Contribution to the Critique of Political Economy* in *Karl Marx: Selected Writings in Sociology and Social Philosophy*. New York: McGraw-Hill.

Marx, Karl. Transl. T.B. Bottomore and M. Rubel. (1964) *Selected Writings in Sociology and Social Philosophy*. New York: McGraw-Hill.

McLuhan, Marshall. (1967) *The Mechanical Bride*. Boston: Beacon Press.

———. (1965) *Understanding Media: The Extensions of Man*. New York: McGraw-Hill.

Meehan, Peter. (2006) "Brewing for the True Believer: Espresso's New Wave Hits Town," *The New York Times*. Sept. 13, Pages D1, D5.

Mick, David, James Burroughs, Patrick Hetzel, and Mary Brammel. (2004) "Pursuing the Meaning of Meaning in the Commercial World: An International Review of Marketing and Consumer Research Founded on Semiotics," *Semiotica*. 152 (1/4), 1–74.

Moloch, Harvey. (2003) *Where Stuff Comes From: How Toasters, Toilets, Cars, Computers, and Many Other Things Come to Be As They Are*. New York: Routledge.

Murray, Janet. H. (1997) *Hamlet on the Holodeck: The Future of Narrative in Cyberspace*. Cambridge, MA: The MIT Press.

Peirce, C.S. (1958). *The Collected Papers of C.S. Peirce*. Vols. 1–6, edited by Charles Hartshorne and Paul Weiss, 1931–5. Vols. 7–8, edited by A. W. Burks, 1958. Cambridge: Harvard University Press.

Propp, Vladimir. Transl. Laurence Scott. (1968) *Morphology of the Folktale*. Austin: University of Texas Press.

Radway, Janice. A. (1991) *Reading the Romance: Women, Patriarchy, and Popular Literature*. Chapel Hill, NC: University of North Carolina Press.

Rapaille, Clotaire. (2006) *The Culture Code*. New York: Broadway Books.

Rieff, Philip. (ed.) (1963) *Freud: Character and Culture*. New York: Collier Books.

Rossi, William A. (1976) *The Sex Life of the Foot and Shoe*. New York: Saturday Review Press.

Rubinstein, Ruth P. (1995) *Dress Codes: Meanings and Messages in American Culture*. Boulder, CO: Westview.

Sapirstein, Milton R. (1955) *Paradoxes of Everyday Life*. New York: Premier Books.

Saussure, Ferdinand. de. Transl. Wade Baskin. (1966). *Course in General Linguistics*. New York: McGraw-Hill

Schlosser, Eric. (2005) *Fast Food Nation: The Dark Side of the All-American Meal.* New York: Perennial.

Schwartz, Tony. (1983) *Media: The Second God.* Garden City, NY: Anchor.

Seldes, Gilbert. (1924) *The Seven Lively Arts.* New York: Sagamore Press.

Smith, Hedrick. (1970) *The Russians.* New York: Quadrangle/The New York Times Co.

Solomon, Jack. (1990) *The Signs of Our Times: The Secret Meanings of Everyday Life.* New York: Perennial Library.

Theall, Donald. (2001) *The Virtual Marshall McLuhan.* Montreal: McGill-Queen's University Press.

Thompson, Michael. (1979) *Rubbish Theory: The Creation and Destruction of Value.* New York: Oxford University Press.

Thompson, Michael, Richard Ellis, and Aaron Wildavsky (1990) *Cultural Theory.* Boulder, CO: Westview.

Todorov, Tzvetan. Transl. Richard Howard. (1981) *Introduction to Poetics.* Minneapolis: University of Minnesota Press.

Van Tassel, David and Robert W. McAharen. (Eds.) (1969) *European Origins of American Thought.* Chicago: Rand McNally.

Wildavsky, Aaron. (1982) "Conditions for a Pluralist Democracy or Cultural Pluralism Means More Than One Political Culture in a Country." Unpublished manuscript.

Winick, Charles. (1995). *Desexualization in American Life.* New Brunswick, NJ: Transaction.

Weber, Max. Transl. Talcott Parsons. (1958) *The Protestant Ethic and the Spirit of Capitalism.* New York: Scribner's.

White, Donald (1980). "Office Life: Executives Can Lose by a Hair," *The San Francisco Chronicle,* December 20.

Williams, Raymond. (1977) *Marxism and Literature.* Oxford: Oxford University Press.

Wollen, Peter. (1972) *Signs and Meaning in the Cinema.* Bloomington: Indiana University Press.

Index

Adamy, Janet, 130
advertising
    desires are infinite, 52
    exposure to by Americans, 53–54
    Jean Baudrillard on, 46–47
    John Berger on, 52–53
    Marxist theory and, 45
    size of industry, 53
    statistics on, 53–54
Alpini, Prospero, 118
Alsop, Ron, 42
*American Dimension: Cultural Myths
    and Social Realities*, 151
American Mercury, 176
American Mythologies, 13
al-Atassi, Dena, 145

Bagels
    bagels and lox Jews, 153
    imitation bagels, 152
    and Judaism, 151
    origin of, 151
    symbolic significance of, 152
Bally, Charles, 5
Barber, Benjamin, 33
Barbie Dolls
    denotative and connotative
        meanings, 16
Barnes, Susan B., 164–165

Barthes, Roland, 12–13, 116,
    159–162, 178
Baudrillard, Jean, 46–48, 50–51
    on advertising and consumer
        cultures, 46, 47
    postmodern theory and, 47–48
Baxter, Richard, 38
beer
    beer cultures and wine
        cultures, 142
    light beer, 143
    oldest alcoholic drink, 141
Berger, Arthur Asa, 122–125,
    129–130
Berger, John, 52–53, 137–138
Bergman, Ingmar, 98
Bernays, Edward, 35–36
Bernstein, Basil, 26–27
Bikinis
    birth of in Paris, 136
    Britney Spears and bare
        midriffs, 137
    John Berger of nude vs. naked,
        137–138
Blonsky, Marshall, 13–14
*Bloom's Morning: Coffee, Comforters,
    and the Secret Meaning of
    Everyday Life*, 122
Bowen, John, 75

brands
    brand extensions, 110
    claims to distinctiveness, 79
    and commodities, 79
    defined, 75
    functions of fashion, 76–77
    impression management and, 112
    as "objets d'art," 111
    self and, 182
    semiotics and, 78–80, 111–112
    status symbols and, 77
Brands: The Logos of the Global Economy, 68, 80, 118
Brand Strategy, 99
Brasch, R., 141–142
Braudel, Fernand, 117–118, 149
Brenner, Charles, 98–99
Bretonne, Rétif de la, 106
"Brewing for the True Believer: Espresso's New Wave Hits Town," 119
Briggs, Asa, 134–135
Burros, Marian, 12

Calvin, John, 36–39, 41
Campbell, Colin, 61
Campbell, Robert Jean, 106
Captains of Consciousness: Advertising and the Social Roots of Consumer Culture, 35
Carroll, Jon, 155
Chandler, Daniel, 24–26
Chase, Marilyn, 90
Childhood and Society, 108
Cinderella, 105
codes
    and culture, 23–27
    imprinting and, 23–24
    kinds of, 25–26
    restricted and elaborated, 26–27
Coen, Robert, 53
coffee
    calories in Starbucks, 122
    consumption of in America, 118
    Dunkin' Donuts and, 120
    new wave coffee houses, 119, 120
    origins of, 117
    Starbucks' impact, 119
    Starbucks' innovations, 121
Collected Papers of Charles Sanders Peirce, 9
Collective Search for Identity, 76
Computer-Mediated Communication: Human-to Human Communication Across the Internet, 164
computers
    communication facilitators, 166
    email and emotions, 166
    ethical questions and, 167
    impact on our lives, 166
    as tools and communication devices, 167
Consumed: How Markets Corrupt Children, Infantilize Adults, and Swallow Citizens Whole, 33
Consumer Culture & Postmodernism, 55
consumer cultures
    Baudrillard on advertising in, 46–47
    capitalism and, 34
    connotative differentiation, 7
    defined, 34–35
    greed and, 40–42
    impact of John Calvin's theology, 36–39
    Marxist theory and, 42–46
    material culture and, 34
    pressures on people in, 51
    Protestant ethic and capitalism, 37–39
    psychological imperatives of, 40–42
    sacred origins of, 36
    and shaping identity, 33
    shaping people's thinking, 35–36
Consumer Cultures & Postmodernism, 34

Consumer Reports, 147
Consumer Society: Myths and Structures, 50
Core Sociological Dichotomies, 47
cornflakes
   cereal as candy, 147
   Post Shredded Wheat diet, 148
   sugar in packaged cereals, 147
   ubiquitous nature of, 146–147
Course in General Linguistics, 5, 20–23
Coward, Rosalind, 15
Culler, Jonathan, 4, 6
Culture Code, 22–23
Custine, Marquis de, 139

Danesi, Marcel, 27–28, 111
"In Defence of Shopping," 60
Dichter, Ernest, 56–57, 58, 61
Digital Dialectic, 94
Dokoupil, Tony, 103–104
Douglas, Mary, 58–61, 157, 177
Dress Codes: Meaning and Messages in American Culture, 102
Drucker, Peter, 68, 69

"Eating Well Notebook," 122
Eco, Umberto, 11, 12, 29–30
An Elementary Textbook of Psychoanalysis, 98
Ellis, John, 15
Empire of Signs, 178
"The Enamel Cult," 93
Erikson, Erik H., 108
"Evangelical Hamburger"
   dynamics of McDonaldism, 130
   McDonald's and evangelical religions, 130–131
Ewen, Stuart, 35

facial hair in men
   beards as signs, 95–96
   products for trimming, 96
   signifier of masculinity, 96

Fairclough, Gordon, 130
Falk, Pasi, 61
fashion
   and identity, 76–77
   Simmel on, 77
Fast-Food Nation: The Dark Side of the All-American Meal, 131
Featherstone, Mike, 34–35, 55, 181
Ferdinand de Saussure, 4
Ferdinand de Saussure Revised Edition, 6
Fey, Tina, 31
Forbes Life, 92
Forbes Magazine, 103
Ford, Tom, 107–108
Fortune, 120
Forty, Adrian, 162–163
fountain pens
   loss of popularity, 135–136
   origins of, 134
   rollerball pens and, 136
fragrances
   brand narcissism, 98–101
   "Consumer Narcissus," and, 99–101
   L'Oréal case study, 100–101
   perfume's erotic mission, 97
   semiotics of perfume names, 97–98
Frederick, Christine, 163
French-fried potatoes
   consumption in America, 133
   role in obesity problem, 133
Freud, Sigmund, 29, 53, 57, 83–84, 108–109
Freud: Character and Culture, 83
furniture
   couthification and, 158
   cultural alignments and, 157
   house a symbol of femininity, 156
   unconscious involved with choice of, 157

games and exercises
  automobiles and personality,
    172–173
  insights learned from book, 174
  socio-economic classes and brands,
    171–172
  spending spree, 173
  time capsule game, 169–170
  visit America brochure, 170–171
  your brands and what they
    reveal, 171
Garber, Marjorie, 143–144
Geertz, Clifford, 14–15
*A General Introduction to
  Psychoanalysis*, 108
Giedion, Sigfried, 123–124, 148–149
Goffman, Erving, 91
Gorer, Geoffrey, 126–127, 140
Gorney, Roderick, 30
Gottdiener, Mark, 4
grid-group theory
  consumption based on lifestyle,
    60–61
  four lifestyles, 59–61
  shopping is agonistic, 61

hair
  blondeness, 87–88
  folklore and myths, 85, 86
  money spent on, 84–85
  semiotics and hairstyles, 86–87
*Hamlet on the Holodeck: The Future of
  Narrative in Cyberspace*, 153
handbags
  behavior of schoolgirls in
    Japan, 107
  externalization of female sexual
    organs, 109
  important fashion accessory
    now, 107
  Tom Ford on, 107–108
Handbags: The Power of the Purse, 107
*Handbags: What Every Woman Should
  Know*, 107

Harper's, 125
Hinsie, Leland E., 106
Hippocrates, 4
History and Human Survival, 8
Holmes, Sherlock, 29
How Did It Begin?, 141
Huizinga, Johan, 115, 182
Human Agenda, 30

Interpretation of Cultures, 14
iPod, 114, 179

Jenks, Chris, 47
Johns, Brad, 88
Johnson, Anna, 107
Johnson, Lois Joy, 88
Johnson, Mark, 17, 19

Kawasaki, Kazuo, 89
Klapp, Orrin E., 76–77
Klein, Melanie, 40
Kotler, Philip, 56, 75

Lakoff, George, 17, 19
*Language and Materialism:
  Developments in Semiology
  and the Theory of the
  Subject*, 15
Lawrence, D.H., 88
Lifton, Robert Jay, 8, 9
Linn, Allison, 119
Linton, Ralph, 176
Love, Hate and Reparation, 40
Lunenfeld, Peter, 94
Lury, Celia, 68, 80, 118–119
Lutens, Serge, 97
Lyotard, Jean-François, 49, 50,
  112–113

Makens, James, 75
Marcos, Imelda, 106
Marcus, Stanley, 157–158
Marketing for Hospitality and Tourism,
  55–56, 75

marketing theory
  Claritas PRIZM groups, 63–68
  Claritas typologies, 62–68
  demographic approaches, 61–68
  Dichter and motivation research,
    56–58
  Drucker on, 68
  grid-group theory and, 58–61
  New Strategist publications,
    61–62
  psychological approaches, 56–58,
    see also psychoanalytic theory
  semiotics and, 69–71
Marx, Karl, 42–45, 46
Marxism and consumer cultures
  alienation all-pervasive, 44–45
  base shapes superstructure
    theory, 3
  role of advertising critical, 45
  society shapes consciousness, 43
McCain, John, 104
McDonald, Mac, 32
McDonald, Richard, 132
McLuhan, Marshall, 12, 178
Mechanical Bride, 12, 178
Mechanization Takes Command,
  123, 148
Media Semiotics, 111
Media: The Second God, 19
Medusa, 85–86
Meehan, Peter, 119
metaphor
  "love is a game" implications, 18
  relation to metonymy, 16–20
  and simile, 16–17
Metaphors We Live By, 17
metonymy, 16–20
Milne, A.A., 159
Minnesota Daily, 129
Moloch, Harvey, 116
More, 88
Morley, Jeffrey, 90–91
Morocco, 144
Murray, Janet H., 153–155

Myst
  benefits of video games, 156
  immersive nature of video games,
    155
  problems with video games, 155
  Riven and, 154
  sales of, 154
  size of video game software
    industry, 155
Mythologies, 12, 13, 159, 160

neckties
  categories of necktie wearers,
    102–103
  optimism and pessimism and, 103
  prices of, 103–104
  as signs, 101–102
"The New Hair Color Rules," 88
New People, 87
Newsweek, 30
New York Times, 119, 122, 145

Obama, Barack, 104, 114, 175
objects and artifacts
  aesthetic sensibilities and, 177
  complexity of, 177
  importance of sign values of, 179
  iPod Shuffle and the pastiche,
    180–181
  lifestyles and choices of, 177
  people watching and, 178
  reflect technological level, 177
*Objects of Desire: Design & Society
  from Wedgwood to IBM,* 162
"One Hundred Percent
  American," 176
Oswald, Laura R., 78–79

Palin, Sarah, 31, 89
Paradoxes of Everyday Life, 156
Paulson, Stephanie, 107
Peirce, Charles Sanders, 4, 9,
  10, 181
"Peirce's Theory of Signs," 10

People of Great Russia: A Psychological Study, 126
A Perfusion of Signs, 9, 10
Popular Culture in the Fifties, 136
Postmodern Condition: A Report on Knowledge, 49, 112
postmodernism
    Baudrillard's theories, 47–49
    de-differentiation in, 113
    defined, 113
    eclecticism and, 113
    Lyotard on, 49–50
    style and identity, 112–114
Preface to a Contribution to the Critique of Political Economy, 42
Presentation of Self in Everyday Life, 91
Protestant Ethic and the Spirit of Capitalism, 37
psychoanalytic theory
    Freud on hats, 83–84
    iceberg as visual metaphor of unconscious, 57–58
    marketing research and, 56–58
    narcissism defined, 98–99
    people unaware of motivations, 57
    shoes and psyche, 104–107
    significance of handbags, 108–109
    soap powders and detergents, 160
    Teddy bears, 159
    topographic theory, 57–58
"Pursuing the Meaning of Meaning," 70
Pyke, Magnus, 145–146

Quigly, Laura, 87

Rapaille, Clotaire, 22–24
Rapunzel, 85
Regelson, Stanley, 151–152
Reiff, Philip, 83
Rickman, John, 126–127
Riviere, Joan, 40–41, 53
Rossi, William A., 104, 105

Rowland, Greg, 47, 69, 97–100
Rubinstein, Ruth R., 102, 103
Russians, 128, 138

Salamone, Frank A., 136
San Francisco Examiner, 119
Sapirstein, Milton R., 156–157
Saussure, Ferdinand de, 4–10, 20–22, 181
Schlosser, Erich, 133
Schwartz, Tony, 19–20
Sebeok, Thomas, 9
Sechehaye, Albert, 5
Semiotic Challenge, 116
semiotics
    ancient roots of, 4
    brand extensions and, 110–112
    and brands, 78–80
    "far out" and "far in," 181
    Greek root for, 4
    hairstyles and identity, 86–87
    ideologies and, 15–16
    "It's still with me," 183
    language and speech, 20–23
    metaphor, 16–19
    metonymy, 16, 18–19
    myths and thinking, 15
    Pierce's theory, 9–10
    power of oppositions in mind, 8
    role in interpreting consumer culture, 183
    Saussure's theory of semiology, 4–8
    signs and codes, 24–26
    signs can lie, 11
    studies signs in society, 5
    symbols, 14
    use in studying cultural phenomena, 4
"Semiotics and Strategic Brand Management," 78
Semiotics: The Basics, 24
Sendak, Maurice, 159
Sex Life of the Foot and Shoe, 104

shoes
  Cinderella folktale and, 105
  fetishism and, 106–107
  folktales and, 105
  foot as erotic organ, 104
  podoerotica, 104
  sexual aspects of the foot, 105
signs
  icons, 9
  impersonators, 31
  imposters, 31
  indexes, 10
  meaning of is arbitrary, 5
  no sign as sign, 28–29
  signified as concept, 5
  signifier as sound or image, 5
  signs that lie, 29–31
  signs within signs, 29
  symbols, 10
*Signs of Our Time: The Secret
    Meanings of Everyday Life*, 158
Simmel, Georg, 77
"A Simple Scarf, But Meaning Much
    More Than Faith," 145
Smith, Hedrick, 128, 138–139
soap powders and detergents
  Barthes' classification of,
      161–162
  international capitalism and, 162
  need psychoanalytic
      interpretation, 160
Solomon, Jack, 158–159
Strategy of Desire, 57
*Structures of Everyday Life:
    Civilization and Capitalism
    15th-18th Century*, 117, 149
style
  postmodernism and, 112–114
  stylessness and, 113–114
style choices and identity
  designer eyeglasses and sunglasses,
      88–90
  facial hair in men, 95–97
  fragrances, 97–104

hair, 84–88
handbags and messenger bags,
    107–110
hats, 81–84
neckties, 101–104
semiotics of hats, 82
semiotics of teeth, 90–91
shoes, 104–107
wristwatches, 92–95
*Superculture: American Popular
    Culture and Europe*, 145
swaddling cloths
  Gorer hypothesis, 127–128
  Russian feast/famine behavior
      and, 128
  Russian psyche and, 127–128
System of Objects, 46

Teddy bears
  and innocence, 159
  manifest and latent functions of
      toys, 160
  toys in French society, 159
*Theming of America: Dreams, Visions,
    and Commercial Spaces*, 4
A Theory of Semiotics, 11
toasters
  is toast a product or a process?, 124
  new products for, 124–125
  white bread and, 123
Trophy Kids Grow Up: How the
    Millennial Generation is
    Shaking Up the Workplace, 42

Understanding Media Semiotics, 27
University of Chicago National
    Opinion Research Center, 62

vacuum cleaners
  bagless, 164
  evolution of, 16
  focus on hygiene to sell, 163
  origins of, 162
  technological breakthrough, 164

Valle, Pietro della, 118
veils
    and Muslim religion, 144
    as signifiers of the female, 143
    signify danger now, 145
Vested Interests: Cross-Dressing & Cultural Anxiety, 143
Victorian Things, 134
vodka
    deaths from in Russia, 139–140
    popularity in USA, 140
    role in Russian society, 140
Vuitton, Louis, 89

Wall Street Journal, 89, 90, 130
Walsh, David F., 47
Waning of the Middle Ages, 115, 182
Warner, W. Lloyd, 172
Ways of Seeing, 52, 137
Weber, Max, 37–39
Where Stuff Comes From: How Toasters, Toilets, Cars, Computers, and Many Other Things Come to Be as They Are, 116
White, Donald, 86
white bread
    bread revolution in USA, 150
    ethnic breads and, 149
    and ideology hypothesis, 150–151
    malleability of, 149
Wildavsky, Aaron, 58–59
Winick, Charles, 16, 87–88
Wired, 155
wristwatches
    cost of expensive watches, 92–93
    digital watches, 93–95
    digital watches and alienation, 94–95
    important fashion accessory, 92

"Your Suit is Pressed, Hair Neat, But What Do Your Molars Say?," 90

Zeman, Jay, 9, 10